Royal Entertaining & Style

First Published in October 2010
Reprinted March 2011
Second Reprint January 2012
Third Reprint February 2013

Text copyright: Ingrid Seward
Pictures: Press Association Images
Design copyright: Mpress (Media) Ltd
Editor: Joe Little

ISBN: 978-0-9567015-1-0

Published By:
Rex Publications Ltd
64 Charlotte Street London W1T 4QD
Tel: 020 7436 4006 Fax: 020 7436 3458
www.majestymagazine.com

Designed and Printed by mpress
Unit Four, Ashton Gate, Harold Hill, Romford, RM3 8UF Telephone 01708 379 777

Contents

MY INVOLVEMENT WITH *Majesty* magazine for the last 27 years has given me the opportunity to meet and talk with hundreds of interesting and influential people including, of course, the royal family. Over time I have witnessed the changes within their staffs and households, but the thread of their lives remains essentially the same.

They have a precise and unchanging routine that has been observed for years, partly because the Queen herself is such an immaculate creature of habit. Her staff say they can set their watches by her, from the time when, after her morning bath, she sits down to breakfast in her private dining room, right through to when her maid draws her second bath of the day before bed. Like millions of her subjects, the Queen finds that an evening bath is relaxing and helps her to sleep.

Royal Entertaining and Style reveals how the royal family lead their lives and how they like to entertain in the great royal palaces and castles, as well as in their private homes.

The House of Windsor is a close-knit clan, constantly renewing themselves by marriage. Newcomers are drawn in and become engulfed by royal life, all personal freedom gone. It is a big price to pay, but there are compensations – notably a life of unique luxury enriched by many perks and the privilege of being a part of history.

This book is about those lives, and is the first of many *Majesty* specials.

Royal Style

T HE BRITISH ROYAL FAMILY are amongst the most privileged people in the world. They live in a collection of palaces, castles and beautiful homes, surrounded by an incredible number of treasures and works of art. Many of these treasures they do not own, but they have the day-to-day use and enjoyment of them. But for all their wealth they are very much prisoners of their position. They are waited on hand and foot by a huge staff of servants – during the summer holiday in Balmoral there will be around 120 staff to look after perhaps a dozen people – though, to be fair, the royal family never use the word 'servant', considering it demeaning. They call those who work for them in a domestic capacity 'staff'.

Protection officers, chauffeurs, pages and older, long-serving staff are all called by their Christian names. However, the royal family are addressed formally: 'Your Majesty' (the Queen) or 'Your Royal Highness', never 'Ma'am' or 'Sir'. Everyone who works for them has a definite function, and the end result is that they are cosseted from the moment of their birth.

On a higher level than the staff, a team known as the Royal Household deal with the Queen's engagements, both public and private, money matters and much, much more besides. It is possible that neither the Queen nor Prince Charles has ever signed a cheque.

For all their vast wealth, the royal family do not lead lives of extravagant luxury, although, like the rest of us, those who do fascinate them. They rarely travel for pleasure. They are at their happiest on the Queen's estates, Balmoral in Aberdeenshire for their summer holiday, or at Sandringham in Norfolk where Her Majesty and Prince Philip spend approximately six weeks in the winter. Actually they are content anywhere in the country surrounded by horses and dogs and they enjoy the traditional country pursuits of shooting and fishing.

Only the younger members of the family can be found on ski slopes and tropical islands. Even Prince Charles, who enjoyed his annual skiing holiday at Klosters in Switzerland for many years, has not been recently as he does not want to appear ostentatious in times of recession.

With a few exceptions the royal women are uninterested in designer fashion. They spend their money as if every penny were their last and Princess Anne still wears outfits she has had for over 30 years, seeing no reason to discard them if they fit and are in good condition. Since her marriage, the Duchess of Cornwall has largely ditched her jeans and wax jackets and now dresses in a suitably regal fashion, not dissimilar to that of her mother-in-law.

The Queen's clothes are the domain of her personal assistant and senior dresser, Angela Kelly. Originally from Merseyside, Angela is responsible for the workroom at Buckingham Palace, which includes a seamstress, embroiderer, milliner and a team of assistant dressers.

As is traditional with a senior dresser to the Queen, Angela coordinates the appointments with couturiers and keeps a tight rein on the whole production. She prides herself on sourcing all the fabrics, often using material that has been in the palace for years or that she has gathered from her travels with the Queen. After the materials have been chosen, the sketches for outfits are submitted, changes made when necessary and then returned to the designer. Recently Angela has been designing under her own label 'Angela Kelly' and the clothes are made on the Dresser's Floor at Buckingham Palace. Because they are created 'in house' they are obviously much less expensive to produce.

Estimates for outfits from other designers are always submitted to Angela, who gets them approved before anything is made up. The Queen insists on paying the same as everyone else and will not accept gifts of clothing.

Miss Kelly's assistants log everything that the Queen wears, including jewellery, shoes, handbags and hats, into a daily diary; if one gets lost there are back-up copies, all written neatly by hand. They are historical documents reflecting the everyday life of the sovereign and will eventually be stored in the Royal Archives. Even in this subdued age of casual dressing, royalty still have to dress like royalty and the Queen has perfected the art of dressing smartly without appearing flashy or overdressed.

The royal family have no snobbery at all about their subjects and in their dealings with people they rarely put a foot wrong. Their perfect manners are inbuilt by Nanny from childhood, thus the deportment and decorum of royalty is learnt by rote. If they are going to involve themselves in a rumpus it is usually with their own kind and in private.

Many years ago Prince Charles left his valet a note telling him to ask the chef to make two big catering tubs of custard. He wanted them to be ready by 5pm as he was going to take them to Lady Sarah Keswick's very grand home in London's Holland Park, where she lived with her parents. Lady Sarah is an old friend, and he is now godfather to one of her children. The chef was not told what the custard was for. It all had to be handled very discreetly, as Lady Sarah was going to have a custard pie fight at her house. Unfortunately, the pastry chef cooked superb custard, thinking it was for eating, not throwing.

The Prince transported the two tubs – still warm – in the back of his Range Rover. And when it was thrown it had still not cooled: it therefore made the most appalling mess. Lady Sarah's father, Lord Dalhousie, then the Queen Mother's treasurer, was furious. The dining room had to be redecorated.

But this rather juvenile behaviour usually only happens in the cosy confines of their own set. Apart from occasional outbreaks – such as those once attributed to Princes William and Harry – in private, the royal family have an old-fashioned, easy-going style. Their aim is to be comfortable themselves and to see that the people around them are equally comfortable and at ease.

Prince Charles is always particularly concerned that, when in public, those around him are not embarrassed. Years ago he went to a function given for a Third World leader. Suddenly the guest of honour began to drink from his finger bowl. There was the sound of sniggering around the table and a few nudges, but when Charles saw what was happening he too picked up his finger bowl and did the same. The shamefaced guests then followed suit.

In private, the royal family sometimes do laugh at the gaffes of the *hoi polloi*. One of the late Princess of Wales's favourite family stories concerned attending a James Bond film premiere. It took place before her wedding, when she was still Lady Diana Spencer.

She was seated next to the star of the movie, the debonair Roger Moore, who, every time he turned to speak to her, surreptitiously used a mouth freshener. But the future Princess was well aware of what was going on as she could hear the continual hiss of the spray and smell the pepperminty scent of the stuff.

She pretended not to notice, because members of the royal family would feel they had failed in their duty if they caused embarrassment to anybody. They try to practise the simple courtesies of never being late or forgetting names.

Of course, they are always well briefed beforehand, particularly if it is someone they have met before. Also, their equerries and ladies-in-waiting are trained to soothe people's nerves before being presented to them, since people do get very nervous. As a result it is rare for anyone presented to the Queen to be able to remember exactly what she said once she has moved on.

Their good manners are not just for the public. The royal family rarely use four-letter words. Prince Philip has been known to shout at people, and the word 'bloody' allegedly figures in his vocabulary. 'Bloody' is also the Prince of Wales's strongest expletive. The Queen's strongest word is 'fool', but shouting at people is not one of her habits. Prince Charles has a very quick temper and is a renowned object thrower when he loses it.

His former butler Paul Burrell had a book hurled at him, but it missed and the Prince ranted and raved at the unfortunate chap, only to apologise profusely afterwards.

The Queen would never do such a thing, however. While the monarch shows respect to her subjects, she is equally punctilious about the way that people approach her and her family. She insists that none of the centuries-old rules on dealing with the monarch is ever broken – not out of any feeling of personal grandeur, but because she is the embodiment of the Crown and respect must always be shown to the Crown. Although rules on curtseying

and bowing have been relaxed, no one sits in the Queen's presence without being invited to do so. There are only a handful of people in the world who call her by her Christian name.

Some of these formalities can cause some difficulty on occasions. An unwritten and very awkward rule about dining with the Queen is that, once seated, no one is supposed to leave the table until she does. It is considered very bad form to leap up and head for the lavatory in the middle of the meal: nature must be attended to before sitting down.

But there was an occasion at Sandringham when, following tradition, the local clergyman who was to preach at the weekend was invited to dinner. Deeply embarrassed, he explained to the Queen's equerry that he would like very much to be present, but that he suffered from a weak bladder and might well have to excuse himself during dinner. The Queen instantly relayed a message that this was of no consequence and everyone would quite understand.

However, she mentioned the parson's difficulty to no one else, feeling that his health problems were nobody's business but his own.

The first time he excused himself from the table over dinner nobody said a word, except for Princess Margaret who looked around the table and said, puzzled, 'Where's he going?' No one answered her.

The second time he went she asked 'What is he up to?' in outraged tones, believing he was slighting her sister.

'Do be quiet,' the Queen said. 'He's going to the loo.'

It was such an unusual thing to happen that the other guests couldn't help but stare at the poor man when he tried to slip back unobtrusively into his place.

The Queen is terribly superstitious about the number 13. If there are unexpectedly 13 for a meal (say the clergyman is invited rather late in the day, which does happen sometimes, or if someone is unavoidably delayed), the dining table will be laid up for ten only. At one end another smaller table will be laid for three people, with a three- or four-inch gap separating it from the main table. So in effect there are two tables, one for three and one for ten.

Even if there is only one person present who is not a member of the family, protocol would demand not only that no one would leave the table while the Queen was sitting, but that no one would sit before she sat, and that she would be served first. Interestingly, both the Queen and the Duke of Edinburgh used to insist that Queen Elizabeth the Queen Mother was treated as number one guest and served first when she was present on family occasions. And they prefer round tables, which solve any protocol problems.

The royal family always go to enormous lengths to find out what their guests prefer to eat, and on any large occasion they play safe with the simplest of meals. After all, it's not everyone who enjoys snipe on toast for breakfast, as Prince Philip does – particularly when he has shot it himself. They like their hosts to be equally careful, but like any polite guest, all members of the royal family will eat what is put in front of them.

Prince Charles dislikes chocolate in any form when served as a pudding and it is astonishing how often chocolate mousse, chocolate cake or chocolate sauces are served to him. When given snake in Hong Kong, he ate it and muttered: 'The things I do for England.' It's not surprising that he himself says he has a cast-iron stomach.

'When I ate raw squid in Japan', he once said, 'it tasted like chopped up garden hose. We ate very strange food in the Far East: things like octopus. But the sight of all those suckers was rather revolting. I wouldn't like the idea of sheep's eyes... maybe if I could swallow them in one go! It is probably the thought of having to chew them that puts me off. But I'm quite prepared to try anything once.'

Even so, all they want is that people ask questions first – and it's quite simple. Should for instance Charles and Camilla be coming to a meal at your home, the routine is to ring up their private office and request guidance on what to serve.

The royal family always get it right for their guests. When a former Chief Rabbi went to lunch at Buckingham Palace, he insisted on bringing his own kosher chef, much to the royal chef's annoyance. The man was brought from a Jewish restaurant in London's Soho and, apart from cooking, he had to serve the rabbi personally. Without making any fuss about security, the Queen permitted him to come into the dining room. It is hard to imagine many other countries allowing a stranger into the presence of their head of state. The Queen simply accepted the situation on religious grounds, as she does with Arab guests and their customs. She continues to serve alcohol at banquets when she has guests from Islamic countries, but they are not expected to drink it. Jugs of orange juice are always placed by them at table. What they drink in their own rooms is their own business, but in front of the world, at the Queen's banquet, they must be seen to be drinking fruit juice.

Some of the requests that the royal family receive from their guests do create small difficulties. When the late Emperor Hirohito of Japan came on a state visit his food was enough of a problem, but an even bigger one was that it all had to be served tepid. As the entire system at the palace is dedicated to serving hot food, this was not easy to achieve. In the end the silver dishes containing his food were left off the hot plate and allowed to cool down naturally.

Many people imagine that the Queen and her family live on caviar, foie gras and champagne. In fact, nothing could be further from the truth. The royal family do not spend their money on great delicacies, nor does one hear or see many champagne corks popping about their homes. In an effort not to appear extravagant, they have even cut out champagne at diplomatic receptions. Guests would probably not be disappointed in the food that the Queen serves but might be surprised at its simplicity.

This is not to say that the royal family do not enjoy the opportunity of eating the kind of food that they never buy for themselves. The huge biscuit-tin-sized container of caviar that the late Shah of Iran sent to the Queen every December as a New Year gift was regarded as a great treat. The Queen would save it for a first course when there were 14 sitting down to dine at the Sandringham winter holiday. The caviar was served in its tin, placed in a silver bowl set into another bowl of crushed ice. The chef would prepare toast, chopped onion and chopped hard-boiled egg with muslin-wrapped chunks of lemon to eat with the extravagant delicacy. Each guest had a heaped tablespoonful, and there were never any leftovers.

Earl Mountbatten of Burma, Prince Philip's uncle who was murdered by the IRA in 1979, was also a recipient. Every New Year the Iranian ambassador would send him a similar tin, which he kept at his home, Broadlands, in Hampshire. His special favourites, including Prince Charles, would be invited upstairs for a secret feast before lunch.

The royal family are astonishingly self-sufficient. They catch their own salmon and shoot their own game and venison. They raise their own chickens and turkeys, and their Christmas trees come from their own forests at Windsor and Sandringham. They eat their own free-range eggs and their own fresh vegetables, grown all year round on the royal farms. The royal family never eat anything tinned or frozen. Their staff, on the other hand, do. What is fresh is reserved for the family.

They grow their own flowers in the glasshouses at Windsor, where they also have their own mushroom farm. But many of these activities are mainly business ventures, something that the Duke of Edinburgh fails to remember if he asks for mushrooms and the chef says he hasn't any in the kitchen.

'What do you mean?' the Duke can shout. 'There's acres of them out there!'

The chefs allegedly do suffer from Prince Philip's wrath. On one occasion he had being visiting in Windsor Great Park and came home with two globe artichokes that he had been given. Deciding they would make a perfect light supper for him and the Queen, they were sent down to the kitchen to the young chef on duty.

Normally artichokes are served as a separate course at the royal residences – they call them a dressed vegetable. So the young chef took all the leaves off, threw them away and cooked just the hearts. These arrived beautifully presented under a silver cover, but there wasn't a great deal left to present. The Duke was not amused.

Much of the produce from the Windsor and Sandringham estates goes to market or the ever-popular royal farm shops. In any case some items, like blackcurrants, are produced in such quantities that the royal family couldn't possibly eat them all themselves. At Sandringham they grow their own peaches, a much-sought-after delicacy and definitely reserved for the family. Boxes of mangos, a great favourite of Prince Philip, are sent to them regularly by the Indian government, and the mangos, like the caviar, are always served on a bed of ice.

The Queen chooses the day's meals from what is called the 'menu book'. This is a small, leather-bound red book with a pencil that runs through the front that also acts like a latch. The book contains the chef's suggestions, which he inscribes in his best handwriting and his best French every morning before the book is presented to Her Majesty by her page. She uses the book for guidance to decide the meals for the day, crossing out the dishes she doesn't fancy.

They have funny rules about fruit. When served, it is always the last course, after the cheese, and called dessert. If the Queen is lunching alone upstairs she always has fruit on her own table. At Balmoral or Sandringham she never serves fruit at lunch, saving it for dinner, though a fruit bowl is always on the breakfast table to be eaten without any pomp. Guests take a knife and an apple and get on with it. At dinner, the eating of fruit becomes a great ritual involving a special dessert service – gilt knives, forks and spoons, and crystal bowls in which it is washed.

Prince Philip and his family turn the eating of a piece of fruit into an art form. The Duke will take the 'lid' from the ripe pear and gently scoop out the flesh until by the time he has finished all that is left is the skin, with the lid placed at the side. They cut all soft fruit round with a smooth-edged gilt knife, twist them and then take the stone out before peeling. Bananas are avoided because they are too filling. When eating grapes, which are always included in the fruit bowl, they take the pips and skin from their mouths very discreetly.

The royal table manners are standard British: they eat with their knife in the right hand, the fork in the left. And most of them eat quite quickly. Prince Charles used to drive his father mad because he is such a slow eater. Normally the staff hand cream and sugar when it comes to serving the pudding, but because the Prince is so slow the footmen leave the jug and bowl beside him for when he gets round to it.

Surprisingly, the food at the palace is sometimes not as good as a top restaurant would serve, which might send Prince Philip stomping off to the kitchen to give everyone hell. But then providing food for the royal family is rather like running a restaurant and serving constantly varying numbers. At one time the Queen employed two head chefs – the royal chef and the staff chef. The royal chef cooked food for about 20 or 30 people, while the staff chef turned out 150 meals a day. Originally all the head chefs were French, and French was spoken in the kitchen. Since the appointment of Ronald Aubery in 1937, the kitchens have been English-run and English is the language spoken in them.

Even today the royal chef never cooks for the staff. That less interesting chore is always left to the younger chefs, while the royal chef keeps an eye on what they are up to. But while the newer recruits are cooking under supervision, they are being trained in royal style. All the chefs throughout the various royal homes have been promoted from being junior chefs at the palace, where they have learned the cuisine that the royal family prefer.

This is a kind of moderated *nouvelle cuisine* – good ingredients, perfectly balanced and attractive to the eye as well as to the palate. Every piece of food is cut to the same size. Each slice of carrot will match the next; each sautéed potato will be of equal thickness and diameter. The little cubes of potato that the royal family enjoy deep-fried are all identical. The food is carefully decorated with greenery or piped sauces – no piece of fish is ever served ungarnished. All the food is prepared by hand, except for mayonnaises and mousses, for which a blender is used.

For state banquets the chef brings in extra help, indeed they call upon the retired chefs, who come with great goodwill – the pay tops up their pensions. Everything is done without stampede or panic.

The royal family have a quite amazing facility for avoiding embarrassing moments, and an equally great gift for ignoring those that do break the even tenor of their lives. Many years ago a drunken footman, who had spent far too long in the staff canteen, dropped a tray of drinks with a resounding crash. It was just as the Queen was receiving her guests at a palace reception. She and the Duke appeared to neither see nor hear what had happened, though the noise caused a momentary hush among the guests present.

Everything is done perfectly, as might be expected. Even the table napkins are folded in a number of different ways. The Prince of Wales's Feathers is one favourite design, but the pantry staff whose job it is to concentrate on the napkins can also make shoes (in which to sit an avocado), flowers, hats – pretty much anything that comes to mind. Some of the napkins do end up awfully creased when opened, though.

Special groups of people are responsible for setting the tables. The Silver Pantry do their part and the China Pantry the rest; then the cellarman supplies the water and the wine, and the Coffee Room the coffee at the end of the meal. Taking into account the chef who cooks the food, and the footmen who serve it, a whole gang of people have been involved in what might be a simple little meal before the Queen has even picked up a bread stick.

The staff are very much part of the pageantry of royalty in that they have different liveries to be worn on different occasions and in different houses. At Balmoral the day-to-day black tailcoat and ordinary, black-trousered livery is worn by both pages and footmen. But to tell the difference between a page (the higher-ranking) and a footman, look out for the pages' dark blue coats with velvet collars, black waistcoats and gold buttons. The footmen sport the same except they have scarlet waistcoats. They wear decorations if entitled to do so.

The footmen wear state livery on state occasions – red breeches, black pumps, scarlet jacket and pink stockings. The white shirt is collarless with a lace frill. The jacket has a black rosette on the back of the collar to commemorate the death of Queen Victoria's husband, Prince Albert, in 1861. It is possibly the same livery that was in use when Albert died. These jackets only come out four times a year, for two state dinners, one diplomatic reception and the State Opening of Parliament. They are put away spotless and get very little wear. A sharp-eyed guest looking beyond the brilliant colour might well spot that the gold buttons sometimes won't meet and the fit is not quite perfect. But this is hardly surprising, as generations of footmen have worn the same jackets and breeches. In the old days, when the royal family had more staff, kitting out the footmen was a bit of a problem. Today there is surplus livery, so it is easier to get a better fit.

Throughout the rest of the year the livery is kept in linen bags, the gold embroidery and gold buttons protected by orange tissue paper that prevents tarnishing. Ruffs are kept in boxes, as are the buckled pumps. One of the livery porters looks after this amazing treasure trove.

Powdered hair was once the absolute rule when state livery was worn. But the powder was just ordinary flour, and incredibly difficult to remove. Flour and water turn into a sticky paste, and the staff used to complain that when they finished work at two in the morning they still had to go upstairs and get rid of the lot. Also, a lot of staff who went bald were convinced that the powdering was the cause. Once they had no hair to powder, they were obliged to wear a wig. Nowadays, moustaches and beards are out: all liveried staff must be clean-shaven.

Things change, but slowly. At Balmoral, well into the late Sixties, the staff still wore the battledress livery adopted by King George VI for the war years. The basic uniform was navy blue; a footman had a red shoulder cord, the pages an embroidered gold flash, and the steward a band of gold on his shoulder, all of which indicated rank. All the battle blouses had EIIR, the Queen's cipher, embroidered on the chest pocket. In the war years the pages and footmen were given military ranks. The pages were made sergeants, the footmen corporals, but since the King's staff were mostly past call-up age, the royal 'regiment' housed some of the oldest sergeants and corporals in the world.

Until recently, footmen were chosen in pairs of the same height, so that they matched exactly when riding on the back of state carriages. In keeping with modern times, women are also now employed in this role.

Liveried staff were never supposed to wear spectacles, and even today they must not be worn when serving dinner. You'd think there would be awful accidents, but there never seem to be. One beautiful hot summer day the Queen and Prince Philip were lunching on the East Terrace at Windsor and the pages and footmen were wearing their white battledress livery – the livery which was worn on the royal yacht. The Queen was quite astonished to be asked by one of her older pages if he could wear sunglasses. He complained that the sunlight hitting the silver salvers and the silver cutlery, not to mention it bouncing off the crystal, was hurting his eyes. He got away with it because he was one of the old-timers, one of those who always had a word of advice for a new recruit. 'Never let them see you enjoying yourself, old boy,' he would say, and it made sense in those more formal days when staff were most definitely seen and not heard.

And yet the royal family are enormously tolerant with their old faithfuls. They are, to a great extent, paternalistic towards those whom they employ. And from their point of view they must not unnerve their staff. Those who are overawed by royalty become inefficient and drop things. All that is required is for the staff to be unobtrusive and stay in the background.

Inevitably, mistakes are made. Once a footman fell in love with Princess Margaret and when he was serving at table he could not keep his eyes off her and blushed and stumbled whenever she was near him. His eyes boring into her eventually drove her mad and he was transferred to other duties. But he was not fired. The royal family like to keep their staff and dislike change, and can be astonishingly forbearing with faithful retainers.

Because of all these helpers, ranging from high-ranking comptrollers and secretaries, through housekeepers, clerks and chefs down to the ordinary rank and file, the royal family are people who live without keys, money, credit cards or even a chequebook about their person. At one time the only thing that Prince Charles and the Duke of Edinburgh ever carried that could spoil the perfect lines of their Savile Row suits was a small silver box containing nothing more exciting than cloves. They carried these in case they were ever served heavily seasoned food, in the belief that chewing a clove clears the breath. The boxes were kept filled with this version of Amplex from the chef's spice box in the kitchen.

The Queen certainly never needs a key to any of her homes. When she is returning to Buckingham Palace, as her car comes down The Mall, followed by a police car, the police communicate with their palace counterparts. The policemen at the gate will stop the traffic, and the page and duty footman will be at the door, as if by magic, at the exact moment that her car drives up.

When the Queen goes to Windsor for the weekend, as she usually does, it is even more of a performance. She leaves from the Garden Gate at the palace for the 40-minute journey. An orderly is already waiting on the Buckingham Palace roof, standing by the flagpole. As her car draws off he lowers the royal standard, and raises the Union Flag. Everyone who can goes too, leaving only a skeleton staff on duty.

When the Queen leaves Windsor again for London, one of her two pages – the one who has been on duty for the weekend – telephones his opposite number in London to say that she has left. And up to the roof goes the flag orderly, keeping an eye out for her car. As it drives through the palace gates, up goes the standard.

As the royal family spend so much of their time in public, when at home they rarely permit themselves to be inconvenienced or disturbed in any way. For example, it is a golden rule that the Queen will not take a telephone call during dinner. There are people she speaks with on a regular basis – people like John Warren, her racing advisor, with news of the next day's racing, particularly if one of the Queen's horses is running. She might also take a call from the kennels at Windsor or Sandringham to say that one of the bitches has had puppies. And certain members of her family have set times to telephone her each week, unless she is abroad.

As Her Majesty once pointed out, the art of being royal is a matter of practice. 'Training is the answer to a great many things,' she said. 'You can do a lot if you are properly trained – and I hope I have been.'

For all the comforts and privilege of the royal lifestyle, few would want such a position. They are indulged, but so are many other people not in the public eye. The royal spectacular might look unchanged from the days when kings made war, but it is an illusion. Nowadays it is more to do with commitment and hard work.

That is royal style.

Fresh Fruit

Scrambled Eggs
Sausages and Bacon
Tomatoes, Mushrooms and Fried Bread

Toast
Croissants

Tea/Coffee

CHAPTER 2

Breakfast with the Royals

BREAKFAST AT ANY one of the royal households is treated with the respect that this first meal of the day is due. The Queen likes to eat in an air of cathedral calm: the early morning is for her the most relaxing time of the day.

Just before nine o'clock a footman hovers in the royal kitchen waiting for the phone call from Her Majesty's page, who has also been hovering just outside her sitting room. When he hears the Queen coming through from her dressing room, he immediately goes to the internal telephone system to summon the royal breakfast. Minutes later, after travelling a few hundred yards, the food is carried on a large silver tray into Her Majesty's private dining room.

The Queen eats breakfast in the company of her husband, Prince Philip, if he is not away. After their early morning cup of Earl Grey tea the royal couple drink coffee – a special blend of their own which comes from the palace coffee room, where the breakfast toast is made. The coffee is freshly ground and served in simple brown earthenware pots that pour from the side. Making this royal brew is a very slow process because the coffee-room ladies use the drip system; boiling water never touches a grain of their special blend, for the royal family believe that it ruins coffee. Yet, conversely, the milk served with it is always hot – the Queen and the Duke drink white coffee at breakfast. The coffee-room staff seem to have got it right, however, as those fortunate enough to have taken coffee at the palace say it is delicious.

The Duke's breakfast-eating habits have changed over the years. There was a time when he had his own electric frying pan, which he kept in the pages' waiting room so that he could rustle himself up some early morning bacon and eggs. Buckingham Palace is so huge that very often food arrives at its destination cold, and the frying pan was the Duke's answer to the problem. Today, like his eldest son, he has turned to a health food diet and his breakfast is more likely to consist of bran flakes, natural yoghurt and honey. The electric frying pan has long been relegated to the kitchen.

When at Buckingham Palace, the Queen and Prince Philip usually eat in the small private dining room that leads off her sitting room. The table is always formally set, with fresh fruit and flowers from the royal gardens placed on brilliantly white linen. There is an electric hotplate on the sideboard to keep food warm.

The Queen never breakfasts in bed, even when on holiday. She considers it a lazy habit, though she does encourage her guests to take their breakfast in their rooms. It gives everyone a little breathing space and time for privacy in the morning. When the Queen stays at other people's houses she always has a tray brought to her room, but even then she doesn't sit and eat breakfast in bed. In fact, it always amazes those closest to her that she only ever allows herself that weakness when she gets a cold. Then she goes straight to bed in order to be well again as soon as possible.

When the Queen is ill and can't keep her appointments, it makes for a great many disappointed people. If any of the family gets anything infectious they are never visited by their nearest and dearest for the same reason.

The Queen used to have a traditional, hearty British cooked meal in the morning – porridge, followed by bacon and eggs or occasionally the special favourite, a kipper. A solid breakfast to start the day is a habit from her childhood, but over the years Her Majesty's tastes have changed and sometimes all she wants is a piece of granary toast and a smear of marmalade.

Tupperware containers with muesli and cornflakes are placed on the table for the Duke – rather than served – so as to avoid waste, and two types of marmalade, light and dark, are provided as well as a carton of yoghurt. When the Queen's younger grandchildren come to stay with her, they are always served a hot meal at 8.30am. Scrambled eggs are a favourite, but this dish is rarely served to adults for breakfast. Once the royal family grow up they prefer their scrambled eggs served with smoked salmon as a light before-the-theatre dish. In the same way, though sausages are always on offer for breakfast for guests, the royal family regard them as a barbecue dish.

The Queen likes to have every one of the national daily newspapers to hand, arranged in a neat fan shape showing each masthead on a small card table beside her while she eats. The Queen always tackles both *Daily Telegraph* crosswords and if she falls behind they are saved and will travel with her wherever she goes until she has time to complete them.

While the Queen and the Duke read the papers, they also have the radio playing softly. Every morning the Queen brings her Roberts radio through from her bedroom and sets it in a corner, tuned to BBC Radio 4.

At the same time her pipe major is at work on the terrace below her dining-room window. He plays Scottish airs for 20 minutes every morning except Sundays – a tradition that goes back to Queen Victoria's day. This is a morning ritual that is so much part of the Queen's day that the pipe major only takes holidays when she is on overseas tours.

If the Queen has been away on a state visit and feels she has put on weight from too many banquets, she will start her breakfast with half a grapefruit. The pastry chef cuts it so each segment can be lifted out with a spoon; he takes out all the pips, and then puts a ring of greaseproof paper on top to stop the fruit from drying out. When the fruit is served – accompanied by a special silver spoon with which to eat it – a page carefully removes the paper.

Meanwhile, at Clarence House Prince Charles and the Duchess of Cornwall eat very little breakfast and, because of their different schedules, they may not necessarily eat together. Camilla will already have been discreetly woken by a gentle tap on the door, announcing the arrival of a butler with a silver tray holding the wake-up cup of tea and freshly-squeezed orange juice. It has to be freshly squeezed, as the couple believe that the vitamins contained in the juice lose their goodness if left overnight in the refrigerator. The Prince doesn't like coffee and never has. Instead, he tries different types of herbal tea, depending on his mood. He has always been a faddy eater and changes his breakfast preferences depending on what he considers healthy at the time. He never uses sugar and always has his favourite honey at hand, even when travelling.

Prince Charles is an early riser and after he has listened to the BBC farming programme on Radio 4 he has his morning bath, drawn by one of his valets, who also lays out a fluffy towel folded in a special way on a chair by the bath so that the Prince only has to step out to be enveloped in its warmth. His valet is the only person allowed in his dressing room and on one occasion when he found a shirt button loose he summoned the valet from his break to attend to it. Once the valet has laid out his clothes (with the socks folded so the royal foot can slip into them) he discreetly disappears while his master dresses.

The Prince and the Duchess have separate bathrooms so that they can bathe and dress in privacy. Camilla is renowned for enjoying a lie in, but the Prince always jumps out of bed as soon as he is awake.

If it seems odd that Charles and Camilla do not breakfast together in London, one has to remember that even when the royal family are all gathered together at the Queen's holiday home, Balmoral, or her weekend home, the vast and rambling Windsor Castle, they rarely take breakfast together. Guests visiting the royal family are treated, well, like royalty. Yet, even so, at Balmoral and Windsor they rarely see the Queen before lunch.

The exception to this rule is when the court is at Sandringham. Every year the court moves to the Norfolk estate for six weeks starting a week or so before Christmas. The emphasis of these weeks is on pheasant shooting, and there is a constant house party of family friends and influential people invited for the sport.

At Sandringham, as at the other royal homes, what they call the morning kitchen is divided. There is the coffee room, which is like an old-fashioned stillroom and deals with continental-type breakfasts and cereals and toasts. Then there is the kitchen itself, which provides cooked breakfasts. It is not a convenient arrangement for the staff: the footmen and pages (usually four of them) have to run between the two to keep the whole thing going.

The Queen and her lady guests all come down to the dining room for breakfast at Sandringham. The enormous selection of breakfast dishes is laid out on the sideboard that runs the length of the room. There is always one main egg dish, accompanied by bacon, plus something fishy – maybe haddock or cod. Occasionally a kedgeree is served, but only when there is leftover salmon. The Queen's favourite kippers are usually on offer.

For those who do not like hot food, there is always a huge York ham on a silver dish with a page waiting to carve. Guests with large appetites manage both hot and cold. Porridge is served with big jugs of farm cream, but guests usually prefer to eat it with fruit picked from the estate.

One of the royals' most delicious – if dreadfully fattening – breakfast dishes is an invention of a long-ago royal chef and it has no name. It is made from a thick slice of bread with some of the crumb scooped out to leave an egg-shaped space. The remaining bread slice is deep fried until crisp and golden, and a perfectly poached egg is then dropped into the centre opening.

When on holiday, if the Duke has shot a snipe the day before, he'll eat it on toast for breakfast. Snipe are such tiny little things, difficult to bring down because they weave about in flight. Prince Charles would never shoot them; he feels sorry for them.

Breakfast is served from 8.30am. On Sundays it is half an hour later so that everyone, including the Queen, gets a bit longer in bed. The meal is always set up the previous night. Immediately after dinner, when the candelabra have been cleared to the silver pantry, the two duty footmen put heat mats and a thick baize cover on the superbly polished sideboard and long dining table. Then everything is covered with a white linen tablecloth before setting plates and cruets. The only time the royal family ever use linen is at breakfast and tea. The spectacular white damask tablecloths and enormous napkins used in the morning belonged to Queen Victoria and are still going strong.

It seems incredible that this wonderful embossed linen has lasted for more than a century, but then one has to remember that it is brought out for only six weeks of the year. The Balmoral linen, also once property of Queen Victoria, is used for ten weeks in the summer. So the table linen lasts much longer than in an ordinary household. Also, it is not beaten about in modern laundries but washed by the staff, whereas the marvellous old linen in London and Windsor goes to a special little laundry in Clapham.

Once a week a black and gold van from the Sycamore Laundry arrives to pick up the week's washing in great old-fashioned wicker laundry baskets. Every item is returned neatly folded between layers of tissue paper. Incidentally, napkin rings are considered very unstylish and are now quite unknown on royal tables, though they were used for the duration of the war to save on laundry bills. Today the linen is used only once before being laundered.

The breakfast china is simple yet still goes back several generations. Present-day royals nearly always eat off china that is marked with an ancestor's cipher. The cutlery is plain silver – gilt cutlery is not used at breakfast time. Neither are fish knives and forks. The royal family never use them, considering them *passé* and really rather vulgar. The table is functional, set for convenience rather than formality. At each place the footman lays a cereal spoon and two sets of knives and forks, one for hot food and one for cold. Fruit plates are found down the centre of the table, with a fruit knife and fork on each plate.

Butter is shaped into little pats in the coffee room by pressing it between two old-fashioned wooden moulds. Some of these imprint a motif, such as a thistle, into the butter, which, of course, is also just at the right temperature to spread easily. The royal family do not like very warm rooms, so although butter is never put in the fridge it doesn't melt too easily. If anyone feels chilly, the Queen suggests they put on another sweater.

There are no finger bowls or flowers on the table. Nor are there any special seating arrangements for breakfast – people settle where they land. The Queen has the only 'reserved' seat, usually at the centre of the table, with her back to the window. There are no visible signs to show where she sits, but her guests are 'regulars' and know the rules.

The fruit from the previous night's dinner will have been rearranged in big silver dishes. Cooper's jams – the brand the royal family always use – will have been emptied into crystal bowls, and honey is served in pots with china bees on the lids. The royal family love honey and although they have their own hives, still collect it from anywhere. When anyone gives either Prince Philip or Prince Charles some local honey they are genuinely thrilled and they always buy it for themselves at the sales of work they like to patronise.

The shoot begins at exactly 9.30am every morning except Sunday, when, so as not to offend anybody religious, there is no shooting. The men – and it is only the men who shoot in the morning – are expected to be ready and on time. The greatest crime in royal eyes is unpunctuality, and the Duke of Edinburgh can become very impatient if he is kept waiting.

In this he takes after King Edward VII, the Queen's great-grandfather, who actually put all the clocks at Sandringham forward by half-an-hour so that the royal shooting parties would have more time to kill more pheasants.

The first thing Edward VIII (later Duke of Windsor) did when he became king was to put the clocks right. He loved shooting, but he needed to make a gesture of his own independence against his father's draconian rule. Royalty can be cavalier with clocks even today. One New Year's Eve at Sandringham, the Queen Mother decided to celebrate early and had the staff put all the clocks forward.

Breakfast is served three-quarters of an hour before the shoot begins and the clever ones get in quickly. The Duke will be at the front door at 9.30am ready to go, Land Rovers with their engines running standing outside. Those who may have stayed up too late have been known to grab a soft bread roll, push a piece of ham into it and eat on the run.

Immediately the guns have gone out, the Queen goes upstairs to her rooms. Her lady-in-waiting takes care of any mail that has arrived, and the lady guests are expected to amuse themselves for half an hour. Some go for a walk; others read the papers.

The reason that the Queen comes down for breakfast at Sandringham and nowhere else is because Sandringham was the subject of an attempt at royal reform in the early 1970s. The Duke had decided that life on this royal estate, the Queen's personal property, was to be streamlined: fewer servants would be employed, everyone would serve themselves with food and even the guests would muck in so as to cut down on the running costs.

'Mucking in' is a favourite royal expression, and one that can strike terror into the palace staff. They know from experience that mucking in generally just means a great deal more work for them.

The changes were short-lived. Not a lot of 'mucking in' went on, but some of Prince Philip's plans did work. In the old days the senior staff and officials were served all their meals by junior staff, just as in a Victorian household. That has finished and staff now serve themselves.

The only other surviving reform is that breakfast is now self-service for the dozen or so guests who are invited at any one time to Sandringham. But there are footmen standing beside the hotplates ready and waiting to lift off lids and put the food on the plates. No one is greedy, because the Queen is irritated if she sees uneaten food left on plates going back to the kitchen. She doesn't mind how much people eat, but loathes waste.

And at Sandringham, always present at breakfast, clustered around their mistress, are the Queen's corgis. It's just unfortunate if any guest does not like dogs or has strong views about their presence at mealtimes. Where the Queen goes her corgis go, the patter of paws making a splendid early-warning system that the monarch is approaching.

The routine is different at Windsor and Balmoral. At Windsor, guests always breakfast in their room, having given their order to the page in charge the night before. They are asked to choose between a cooked and a coffee-room breakfast, which is usually just toast and fruit. The cooked breakfast comes on big silver trays on silver dishes with boiling water set underneath – a necessary precaution, as at Windsor it is not an exaggeration to say that the kitchen can be a quarter of a mile from some of the rooms. Indeed, the late Prime Minister Edward Heath was unwise enough to order boiled eggs for breakfast when he was a guest at the castle. They arrived bullet-hard. He sent them back and tried again. The second lot were equally hard. It is not possible to serve a soft-boiled egg in the bedrooms of Windsor Castle.

At Balmoral, where again everything revolves around sport, the gentlemen come downstairs for breakfast in tweed plus-fours or kilts; the ladies are encouraged to remain in their rooms. The Duke of Edinburgh takes his breakfast with the Queen in her private sitting room. Without the royal presence, breakfast is more relaxed for guests than at Sandringham, but standards are still maintained.

Even though the Balmoral holiday takes place between August and October, Scotland can be freezing cold, and so the Queen provides her breakfasting guests with an electric fire. And if it gets very cold there might be a second fire in the corner of the room. Log fires are reserved for the drawing room.

A British breakfast would not be complete without the newspapers, and the royal newsagent's bill is a large one. They would never dream of watching morning television and like to make sure all guests have a paper to read over breakfast. A couple of full sets are laid out in the dining room for the men. Each lady guest is delivered a paper (not of her choice but whatever is available) with her breakfast tray. After breakfast the footmen gather up the newspapers and place them in the drawing room. Actually, at remote Balmoral the papers arrive so late they often become afternoon reading.

Those who breakfast downstairs have a huge choice of food decided by the chef, ranging from sausages or kidneys to coffee and croissants. Yet no guest of Her Majesty can expect elaborate meals. All the royal family have simple tastes. For example, on Easter Sunday simple boiled eggs are always served, as this is an occasion on which no one but the Queen's immediate family will be present. The chef is forever suggesting something more exciting in the menu book, but the Queen firmly crosses out his choice and writes 'boiled eggs' instead.

The meal is eaten in the Queen's private dining room at Windsor and is one of the rare occasions when the younger royal grandchildren – the Earl and Countess of Wessex's Louise and James, for instance – sit down with the family. Prince Philip always presides over a table decorated with fluffy Easter chicks and little silver paper-wrapped chocolate eggs. Small gifts are also exchanged.

Undoubtedly the reason why the Queen insists on plain boiled eggs for Easter breakfast is because this is the tradition in Britain. Normally a royal breakfast is a much more elaborate affair. The mushrooms and tomatoes served will be home-grown, and at Balmoral the Queen also has free-range eggs from the farms on her estate. These are gathered for the consumption of the monarch, her family and guests, while the staff have ordinary eggs, bought in bulk.

Prince Charles has his little eccentricities and during Lent eats only in the evening, even when he has guests staying. Yet there was a time when he rather enjoyed his breakfasts, and he still does when travelling on the royal train. Nowadays the train consists of a series of purpose-built carriages managed and staffed by Network Rail and used for longer journeys in the United Kingdom. The railway chefs still manage to produce a splendid, piping hot meal in a tiny railway galley.

The train usually stops at a siding overnight, but as a light sleeper the Prince of Wales is constantly woken by police crunching on the gravel as they patrol up and down by the royal carriages. He becomes extremely irritated by this and can't wait to get up and out.

Normally, when any member of the royal family is travelling and staying in hotels, he or she becomes dependent on room service. And this is the reason why the Queen loved the royal yacht or an aircraft of the Queen's Flight. On the yacht and in her own plane she was at home and could control what she ate. For royalty, the trouble with staying in hotels is that they are swamped with food and appalled by the amount served, particularly at breakfast time.

Royalty travel with quite a lot of their own food. The Queen takes her own bottled Malvern water, honey and marmalade, while Prince Charles takes as much organic produce from Highgrove as is possible, including honey – he only eats organic – and anything else depending on what his latest fad is. It is all loaded into an estate car in Tupperware boxes and woe betide if anything should be left behind. On the return journey everything has to be carefully packed up, even the honey, and taken back to Buckingham Palace or Clarence House.

The Prince is suspicious of other people's food and habits so he also travels with his own lavatory seat, which may not be as mad as it sounds. He cannot afford to get ill and by taking his own produce and loo seat he at least has every chance of avoiding infections.

Royal House Guests

THE QUEEN LIKES to entertain, and indeed does a great deal of it. But her style is not to invite a few friends in for dinner or for drinks. Other members of the royal family entertain with one-off dinner and cocktail parties, but when the Queen's friends are invited it is almost always for a long weekend. The exception to this rule is when the Queen's grandchildren invite their friends to meet their distinguished grandparents. They will have sought permission well in advance, of course – no one drops in on the Queen.

She rarely entertains personal friends at Buckingham Palace – only heads of state, dignitaries or visiting royalty. The palace is, to her, no more than an office above which she is forced to live for three or four nights a week. A dinner party or a banquet at Buckingham Palace is rather like the head of a vast corporation entertaining in the boardroom. Therefore, when the Queen has personal guests they are invited to her private homes – Balmoral and Sandringham, or her favourite official residence, Windsor Castle. The ancient castle is also where Her Majesty gives house parties for Royal Ascot week in June.

Most of the other entertaining at this, the largest inhabited castle in the world, is called 'Dine and Sleep'. People whom protocol demands are invited come for dinner, are given a bed for the night and breakfast in the morning, and then sent politely on their way.

To be a personal guest of the Queen is quite a different matter, and in the two main royal holiday breaks of January and August/September the Queen entertains more or less constantly. She usually invites about four to six couples at one time, including the latest girlfriend or boyfriend of younger members of the family. Everyone arrives on the Thursday and leaves after lunch on the Sunday.

The venue in January is Sandringham House in Norfolk for the pheasant shooting, and Balmoral Castle in the summer for grouse and deer. Invitations are sent out at least six weeks in advance, but mostly, it must be said, they are posted to what palace staff call the 'regulars'. These are old friends who are generally asked at exactly the same time each year. The routine is so consistent that they hardly need an invitation at all. The Queen and her family hate change and basically like a quiet life with no great fuss, so they find it more comfortable if they are with people who are not overawed by them.

The atmosphere at both of the Queen's private homes is fairly relaxed. There are no dos and don'ts as their guests know how to behave and are *au fait* with the rules when mixing with royalty. Of course, none of the Queen's friends, however close, would dream of calling her by her first name. Though they may have known her since childhood, they still bow or curtsey when she comes into the room or if they meet her in the corridor; they never leave a room until she does and never sit before she is seated.

Most of the Queen's friends have large homes of their own and are wealthy people, but even for the über-rich to stay with her is a treat. These days all the money in the world cannot normally buy the superb staff and the standard of service which royalty enjoy.

The Queen's visitors are not, as you might expect, provided with transport. They get themselves to the nearest railway station, unless they decide to drive. Most people do drive to Sandringham, which is about 110 miles from London, but those invited to Balmoral are more likely to go by train or plane to Aberdeen, the nearest city to the Queen's Scottish home. Her Majesty will send a minibus to meet them to take them the 60 miles to Balmoral Castle. At one time Rolls-Royces were sent, but the minibus is one of very many economies to have been introduced over the years.

The invitation suggests in an informal way that guests arrive around 6pm in time for drinks. When they alight from their transport outside the double front doors, guests are greeted by the Queen's equerry or lady-in-waiting. The monarch may well meet very close friends at the door herself. Meanwhile the luggage man (who, oddly, is still called 'the coal man') is taking the luggage round to the back door. The coal man's jobs vanished once central heating was installed and his role now is to handle all luggage.

Balmoral has dozens of staff to look after the family, senior members of the Queen's household and her guests; Sandringham has rather fewer. Housemaids who wear black dresses bearing the monarch's EIIR cipher look after female guests. Gentlemen are in the care of tail-coated footmen.

The Queen personally inspects the rooms before her guests arrive, making sure they are properly appointed. She checks that there is water at hand, soap in the bathroom and newly published books for bedtime reading. Publishers send her so many books that there are plenty to go around. She herself shows guests to their quarters at about 7pm, fussing like any hostess to make sure that they have all they need. She then leaves, giving them time to prepare for dinner.

Once in their rooms guests find a little guide on the dressing table that will have been left by either the sergeant footman or the housekeeper. On it will be typed the guests' names, together with the name of the maid and footman looking after them. There is a note on the back of the card which advises about tipping, suggesting that £10 per night's stay is about the right amount. The royals do not want to create inflation, but neither do they want their staff to be under-tipped. Very close friends don't get these instructions, as they know the form. Footmen and maids might look after several people and often finish up with anything between £60 and £100 extra a week. Guests only tip these two categories of staff, which occasionally causes jealousy among chauffeurs and chefs.

By the time the guests are in their rooms, the maid will already have unpacked the luggage and put everything away.

She will also have guessed – and the Queen's maids rarely get it wrong – exactly what the lady will be wearing for dinner that night, and taken the dress and the man's evening clothes away to be pressed.

There will be flowers in the room, fresh fruit and a small dish of Bendick's mints, which are much sought-after by the staff. The popular guest is the one who doesn't eat them, leaving yet another little treat for the footmen and maids. Each room at Windsor, as at Buckingham Palace, is furnished with a small drinks tray on which sit three tiny decanters containing gin, scotch and sherry. These hold about three measures each. Wine is never served in the bedrooms, and only semi-official guests get decanters. For close friends in the private homes there is no alcohol of any kind in the rooms; nervous people have been known to bring hip flasks!

Once guests have changed for dinner, the maid will ask what her lady requires for breakfast, since here it is only the men who breakfast downstairs. Orders are always taken the night before to give the kitchen plenty of time to prepare.

Everyone gets their own bedroom and sitting room, but surprisingly not all will have a bathroom *en suite*. Rooms that do have a private bath and lavatory go to the most important guests and, unlike other households, the most important are the royal family themselves. Members of the family are always given the best accommodation. But there is one exception – the Prime Minister. It is a tradition that he or she is invited for one weekend at Balmoral – usually the first weekend in September, although recently prime ministers only seem to manage one night. The suite the Prime Minister occupies has pictures of all past premiers on the walls, hung on ream wallpaper, which, like most things in the Queen's private homes, dates back to her great-great-grandmama, Queen Victoria. And they still have masses of spare rolls to replace any through wear and tear.

Other guests may have to double up on the washing facilities, and one guest still tells the story of a morning encounter with Prince Philip in the corridor – she in her dressing gown, he in a short towelling robe. Feeling rather silly, she dropped into a deep curtsey to find herself staring at a pair of hairy royal knees.

Even when the rooms do have their own baths, the plumbing at both homes can leave much to be desired. The pipes at Balmoral are ancient; they gurgle throughout the night and also relay sound, so that in some rooms conversations taking place in another part of the castle can be heard quite clearly.

Dinner is at 8.15pm, and thankfully first-time guests are always escorted to the drawing room. It is quite easy to get lost, and the Queen would not wish her guests to be embarrassed by being late. The regulars know the way, of course. And when the younger members of the family bring boyfriends and girlfriends to stay (having been declared *persona grata* during a Sunday lunch at Windsor), their hosts always collect them and guide them to the drawing room.

In his bachelor days Prince Charles took down many likely ladies to dinner. Lady Diana Spencer, Sarah Ferguson and Sophie Rhys-Jones got to know the royal family here, and Kate Middleton, the girl tipped to marry Prince William, has been a lunch guest at Windsor and a weekend guest at several of the private homes, albeit without the Queen being present.

The dining room at Balmoral is very grand, with silver centrepieces depicting Scottish pastimes – such as tossing the caber or putting the shot – on the table. The royal family always dress for dinner when they have guests. It may be sweaters and pearls and sensible shoes for daytime, but the ladies are expected to pull out all the stops in the evening. The men sport a dinner jacket, or, if in Scotland and they are entitled to wear one, the kilt. The Queen takes all her best jewellery to Balmoral with her, and wears it, so guests rustle up the grandest they have too.

The Queen always enters the dining room last at Buckingham Palace and Windsor Castle, the official residences. Everyone else is expected to be in position, standing behind his or her chairs, before she appears. At her own homes she herself leads the guests in from pre-dinner drinks in the drawing room. The page announces that dinner is served immediately the first course is outside, ready to go on the table.

The Queen has already prepared what the royals call a dinner board. We would call it a table plan, and she settles down to organise this once she has had tea. The seats are rotated for each night of a guest's stay, so that everyone gets a chance to sit next to a royal personage. Working this out can be quite a complicated task, but it is one that the Queen likes to do herself. The completed plan is left by the drinks' tray, from which people help themselves, so that people can check where they are sitting.

Guests follow Her Majesty into the dining room quite informally. There's no 'piping in' by the pipe major as there was even in the days when the Queen Mother was chatelaine. But at Balmoral the piper still does walk round the table playing after coffee has been served. The ladies still retire, leaving the gentlemen to their cigars and port for about 30 minutes, before the entire party congregates in the drawing room for after-dinner drinks.

At this point, the guests can either steel themselves to play parlour games – charades is a great favourite – or a new film might be shown. The royal family never switch on the television when guests are present. They enjoy watching it themselves, so the programmes they want to see are recorded by a footman and shown in the afternoons when it's their 'free time' as well as everyone else's.

Nobody goes to bed before the Queen, and she generally says goodnight at about 11.30pm. She still has work to do, going through the contents of the official red boxes that follow her everywhere. This is the time for visitors to escape as well, if they are ready for bed. It was also the time when Princess Margaret would sing and play the piano. Once the Queen left, nobody departed from the room before Princess Margaret, and since she was the night owl of the family it could be extremely late before she would retire.

Guests have to sing for their supper in small ways. At Balmoral, the Queen always gives two ghillies' balls, which all the staff, royal family and guests attend. These are the highlight of the annual visit for the estate workers. The women bring out their long dresses; the men wear the kilt. The Queen wears a tiara and a Royal Stuart tartan sash over her evening dress. Guests, like the royal family, are expected to dance with as many of the staff as possible. Dancing stops briefly at midnight for everyone to enjoy late refreshment.

For the younger royal family and staff, the dancing goes on until two in the morning. Being well aware that people have more fun when she is not there, the Queen will have left much earlier. Then the pace increases and everyone lets his or her hair down.

At all royal homes the day goes in stages that revolve around meals. After breakfast, there is no stopping for elevenses. Mid-morning coffee and biscuits are never served, mainly because the royal family do not eat between meals. Brunch is unknown to them. The Queen likes to go riding sharp at 10.30am and ladies can join her if they wish. Anyone who doesn't ride is expected to amuse him or herself. At Balmoral there are about six horses available, brought up from Windsor by road. The shooting dogs are transported from Sandringham in a small van. At Sandringham there are both stables and kennels, so none of the animals have to come from elsewhere.

After riding, lady guests are expected to be ready to go in Land Rovers to join the shoot, where lunch will be taken at around 1-1.30pm. This will be served indoors in Norfolk, or in the open air in Scotland. The entire meal will have been transported by the staff in a van designed by Prince Philip, which very cleverly keeps hot foot hot and cold food and drinks cold. Alcoholic drinks are also served, though it is frowned upon for the guns to drink anything intoxicating.

The royal family love being outdoors, and every weekday in the summer holidays they eat outside. Even if it's a non-shooting day they'll still have a picnic, and guests are expected to be equipped with wellies and tweeds and not mind the elements. These picnics are very civilised. There's not a lot of sitting on damp grass, as along with the food arrive thick car rugs and shooting sticks, which turn into very basic seats.

Winter shooting lunches at Sandringham are rather more comfortable – generally eaten in estate village halls transformed by tables properly laid up with the royal number two silver, and plain white shooting china that goes back to the First World War. All these plates will have been pre-heated at the house and wrapped in blankets to keep them warm.

Lunch over, the ladies then accompany the shoot, walking behind with the dogs. Sophie Wessex and Kate Middleton have both had shooting lessons from one of the ghillies, but are not considered good enough to join in the main shoot.

Those guests at Balmoral who go out for a day of deer stalking will take a small waterproof lunch bag that they sling over their shoulder. It is terribly important to the staff that nobody goes without their lunch, and the lunch bag is checked off along with the guns and ammunition before the hunters leave for the hills. The bag is packed with a very simple meal: a homemade roll, the top cut off, the crumb scooped out, and then filled with layers of meat. Mutton pies, a traditional Scottish delicacy, plum pudding and something to drink are also provided. The drink is usually ginger beer, lemon refresher or lager, with a small hip flask of whisky to be shared with the ghillie on the hill.

It is a long day stalking, but even so, at Balmoral those with any energy left have the opportunity to pop over to the Dee and fish for salmon. It's surprising how many do. Everyone comes home around 5pm for tea, and then follows what the royal staff call the silent hour, when guests get themselves together for the next innings.

At 6pm the drinks tray is wheeled into the drawing room and once again guests can help themselves until dinner is served. It's very rare for anyone to get drunk, though on the occasions when it has happened the Queen pretends not to notice. But she *has* noticed, of course; she really doesn't miss a thing. If people over-indulge it's usually because, in spite of the Queen's efforts to put everyone at their ease, they're suffering from nerves.

The staff are careful not to give guests powerful drinks, and yet the royal family, if handed a bottle and a glass, pour the most lethal drinks for themselves, perhaps out of inexperience. Prince Charles is known to make lethal martinis, but none of them have to pour their own drinks too often, as there are usually several people on hand to do it for them.

It is considered infra dig when signing a royal visitors' book to write anything other than your name and the dates of your stay. But the Queen Mother, though not wishing for comments, used to be charmed if her guests placed a small photograph of themselves by their signature in her large leather-bound book, now in the Royal Archives.

What very often does surprise first-time visitors is that few of the private royal residences are at all grand. At Balmoral a guest might be taken aback to find the stone-floored entrance hall littered with fishing rods, waterproof clothing, wellington boots and dog bowls. The Queen feeds her dogs there personally.

There is also a collection of ancient bicycles left for anyone who feels like a change of exercise from tramping the moors. The hall is dominated by a bust of Queen Victoria, while in the red-carpeted inner hall is an enormous statue of her husband, Prince Albert, In fact the entrance is a sort of clean but cluttered royal dumping ground and it is certainly not tidied up because visitors might be coming.

At Sandringham the front door opens into the Saloon, a great open area filled with comfortable, squashy furniture – nothing grand at all. Everything is sensible and cosy, with the sort of chairs in which people might fall asleep after a long day in the open air. Inside the door is a large pair of sitting scales, rather like buckets. These were a gimmick of King Edward VII, who liked people to be weighed when they arrived and again when they left to see if they'd eaten well. They don't do it any more these days, except to amuse the children. There are screens around the door to help keep out the freezing Norfolk wind, and there's also a piano, a card table and another table for papers and assorted magazines.

The Queen can sit in the hall at Sandringham, waiting for guests or for the Duke to arrive. When she looks out of the Saloon window, she can see the cars come up the drive. The Saloon goes the height of two floors, with a gallery around it that has little stained glass windows. From her vantage point the Queen can see if footmen are eating her mints or sneaking the odd drink. There is very little privacy at Sandringham.

But it is here, more so than anywhere else, that the Queen joins in the house party. Her idea of relaxing is to do a jigsaw. She always has a huge one going. Nothing modern: she likes a really difficult landscape and she hides the lid and puts it together blind. Her jigsaw is placed on two card tables put together with a thick board on top and lit by two bright table lamps so she can see the colours clearly. The jigsaw is for everybody to do, but people do hold back a bit, especially if there is not much to finish and the Queen is out for a walk. There's an unspoken feeling among guests that she wouldn't be too delighted to find it complete. A house party guest wanting to give the Queen a present could not go wrong with a large, complicated jigsaw. Her Majesty would be delighted with the gift.

After dinner on Saturday night the Queen generally shows her guests a brand-new movie. Everyone is expected to attend, seated in comfortable armchairs in a row of about eight. The Queen sits in the centre, Prince Philip beside her. A couple of sofas form the second guest row. This arrangement is all left permanently in the ballroom at both Balmoral and Sandringham, ready for a royal night at the home movies. At Balmoral stags' heads stare down, while at Sandringham the film is watched alongside Edward VII's huge collection of armour displayed in the ballroom.

It's all very democratic. The house staff are invited, and they sit at the back on old-fashioned canvas director-style chairs; there is no kind of pecking order. Staff and their families from the royal estates are also invited, as are any young children who live nearby. Diana Spencer recalled seeing *Chitty Chitty Bang Bang* several times when she was a child as everyone can watch as long as they are in the ballroom before the Queen arrives.

The Queen's pipe major acts as the projectionist, while the equerry sits in the second row with a buzzer to warn him if the sound is too loud or too low, or if the film needs adjusting. It is, of course, a great privilege to see these films before anyone else. And being in the company of the Queen makes it as exciting as any London film premiere – without the need for expensive tickets.

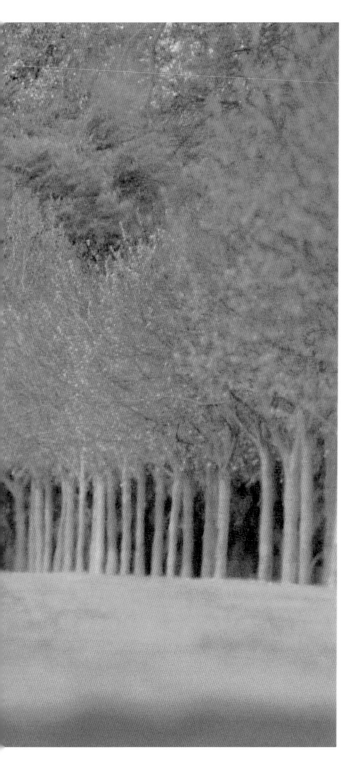

On Sunday, wherever she might be the Queen never misses church. Prince Charles, on the other hand, was once staying with friends who asked him if he wanted to attend the local church or go fishing. He chose to fish, saying: 'I can pray when I'm fishing, but I can't fish in church.' Attending church is not obligatory, but the Queen likes her guests to make the effort.

A royal house party comes to an end after Sunday lunch. After everyone has eaten, the Queen herself guides her departing guests to the drawing room where they are asked to sign the visitors' book. Behind the scenes there has been a lot of activity. While the guests were at church the maids will have packed for them. They first have a good look around the room to see if their guest has left an envelope with the tip. If not, the maid and footman will be hanging around to bid farewell.

Everything will have been laundered. Guests go home as clean as the day they arrived – possibly even cleaner, as some visitors to the Queen's home may have been staying elsewhere beforehand. If they arrive with dirty laundry, it will be whisked away and returned washed and ironed. The men's guns will have been cleaned for them and a brace of birds, boxed for travelling, added to their luggage.

It is not good manners to arrive at any one of the royal homes in a car that looks as if it has been driven through a mud bath, but people do. Yet they will drive away in a vehicle that is polished to within an inch of its life, courtesy of the rarely-seen chauffeurs. That's royal style.

Lunch with the Queen

APART FROM COSY family lunches, which the royals enjoy as much as the rest of us, the midday meal provides another opportunity for the Queen to meet people. She gives several private luncheons a year at Buckingham Palace for up to 12 specially selected guests when she does just that. In terms of the world outside the royal circle, these occasions are rather like boardroom lunches given by a managing director or chairman of a company.

The invitation card sent by the Master of the Household gives at least two months' notice and is almost always sent to their place of work, rather than a home address. This emphasises the 'business' tone of the occasion.

The Queen's luncheon guests are often a motley crew, ranging from jockeys to actors to artists to managing directors of huge corporations. Actress Maureen Lipman has been a guest; BBC TV presenter Terry Wogan was invited; the governor of Britain's largest women's jail was asked, along with people as diverse as editors of the most widely-read newspapers and opera singers. Wives, husbands and partners aren't invited.

These lunches are informal by palace standards but may appear formal to the rest of us. Guests are commanded to arrive at the palace at 12.30pm and are sent stickers for their car windscreens so that they are let through the gates without fuss. A footman then takes them to the Bow Room on the ground floor for pre-lunch drinks, where they are greeted by the Queen's lady-in-waiting and an equerry.

The Bow Room is beautiful, painted cream and gold, but has very little furniture. People who arrive early can inspect the four display cases – one in each corner – that house some of the Queen's priceless collection of china. This is one of the most public rooms in Buckingham Palace, used as a sort of throughway to the summer garden parties. But lunch itself is always held in the 1844 Room next door – the white and gold chamber where the Queen receives visiting ambassadors. Both the Bow Room and the 1844 Room are very formal, not a bit like the royal apartments upstairs, which are littered with dog baskets, books, magazines and family photographs. Few people are allowed to see how the royals really live at Buckingham Palace, and certainly not those who attend the 'Meet the People' luncheons.

On these occasions an oblong table is wheeled into the 1844 Room and set with glittering silver and crystal. Also brought in are two sideboards from which the footmen serve. The palace florist does her bit, and by the time the room is filled with people it looks less austere.

Once all the guests have arrived the Queen comes to join them, just before 1pm, along with the corgis, which stay with her for the entire time. There's no fanfare to signal her arrival, not even an announcement. The door is just opened by the page and suddenly the guests find the Queen and the Duke of Edinburgh among them. There is a fluttering of curtseys and bows, and no one is quite sure what to do with the drink they have in their hand.

The corgis have quite an important function on these occasions as they give people something safe and innocuous to talk about while creating a diversion. On one occasion, many years ago, an old favourite, Heather, was misbehaving, and the Queen snapped sharply 'Heather!' at the dog, thereby making the opera singer Heather Harper, a guest that day, nearly jump out of her skin.

Lunch is served at 1.10pm. The palace steward slips into the room, catches the monarch's eye and says: 'Luncheon, Your Majesty.' The Queen nods and then says casually: 'Shall we go

in, then?' She leaves a few seconds to give everyone the chance to finish their drinks and then leads the way into the 1844 Room. The guests are always fascinated at how relaxed she is; the chances are that they don't feel quite the same. There is a seating plan just outside the room, but if guests haven't spotted it the ever-vigilant equerry or lady-in-waiting points it out so that everyone is seated smoothly.

The Queen always chooses who she wants to sit beside her (the most important male guest will be on her right), while Prince Philip will have a lady guest on his right. People are always surprised to see that the Queen does not sit at the head of the table. Her place on these occasions is in the middle, which seems more friendly, with Philip (or Prince Charles sometimes, if the Duke is away) facing her.

There is a very definite ritual regarding conversation at the table. Throughout the first and second courses, the Queen talks to the person on her right. When the third and fourth courses (pudding and cheese) are served, she turns automatically and chats to the person on her left. She has now 'done' two people, and has perhaps spoken to a couple more in the Bow Room while drinks were being served. She still has a number to go. The point of these lunches is that she has some sort of conversation with all her guests. Sometimes, if the meal is going well and it's a jolly atmosphere, she will talk to people further down the table and a group conversation results.

The polished table used for the luncheons has no linen on it except for napkins (you can be sure that you will never see the paper sort at any of the royal homes). The warmed plates are placed on table mats which carry pictures of the various royal residences, views of Windsor Castle, Balmoral, Buckingham Palace, St James's Palace and so on. Anyone else serving lunch on photographs or drawings of their own homes could be thought to be showing off or even slightly vulgar, but the royals get away with it. Like the corgis and the china, which changes pattern at every course, the Queen feels these are talking points for tongue-tied guests.

Lunch with the Queen

Once seated, the guests begin to relax a little and take in the livery of the serving staff: dark blue tunics for the footmen, while the pages sport tailcoats. Unlike in the old days, no one has to wear a powdered wig or scarlet livery – something that has been known to disappoint some guests. The wigs, abandoned for the war, never reappeared.

The table gleams with King's Pattern silver cutlery, silver cruets and beautiful crystal glass, all engraved EIIR. The Queen has a special pair of cruets for her own use: they are made in the shape of two silver owls and the eyes are the pouring holes. Each guest has a menu in a silver holder. There are no candles on the table at lunch, just flowers arranged in silver baskets. There are no finger bowls, either, and if there were, they would not have bits of lemon or a rose petal floating in them. Prince Charles has been known to give little lectures about these kinds of pretensions.

Hostess or not, the Queen is still the monarch, and when the food is brought around the table on magnificent salvers she is served first. There are two pages serving, and both start in the middle and work their way round.

The Queen prefers to help herself to food, and so the pages who serve present the salver on the left side, with a large spoon and fork,

and wait while the Queen takes what she wants. She will take a very small portion – all the royals eat little but often – and her distinctive voice can be heard after every dish saying 'Thank you'. This is one of the very few times when the Queen actually speaks to the staff when they are on duty, and for a new recruit her clipped but courteous acknowledgement can be quite a thrill.

The guests are served their meal in the same way; there's no question of handing over a plate with food already on it. If anyone is talking too much to spot the waiting page, they are liable to get a little nudge on the shoulder with the salver as a reminder to get a move on and help themselves. While one page is on the left-hand side of the guest, serving, on the right-hand side is the chap pouring Malvern water or white wine. It can get confusing for left-handed luncheon guests.

At these lunches, the staff remain in the room while the guests are eating and clear away immediately there is an empty plate. On other occasions, when the Queen is lunching with friends at Balmoral or Sandringham, the empty plates are all cleared at once. Staff go out of the dining room at these two holiday homes and the Queen rings when it looks as if everyone is more or less finished. Once the staff come in, guests realise they'd better hurry up!

What does the Queen serve her guests? Delicious food of course, but nothing too exotic. Soup is never served at lunch, but the visitors might get a particularly delicate mousse or fish in aspic made in a mould for the first course. One of the Queen's favourite dishes to start lunch is *Oeufs Drumkilbo*, hard-boiled eggs and lobster chopped up and served in a small cup with aspic and a blend of mayonnaise, tomato puree and various sauces.

For the main course traditional dishes are chosen, but curiously never the most traditional British lunch of all – roast beef and Yorkshire pudding. As far as the Queen is concerned this is served on Sundays and no other time. She rarely serves chicken to guests, either, though she herself is very fond of boiled chicken and rice. The royals consider that chicken is nursery food, to be kept upstairs. But there is one exception: she loves a dish called champagne chicken. This is made with a boiling chicken, boned out completely and then stuffed with pâté. Champagne is then poured all over it and it is left to cook slowly. The chef considers this a cheap dish – after all, he does use a chicken from the Home Farm and non-vintage champagne.

The main course at one of these luncheons will probably be either lamb or a veal dish. The Queen herself is very partial to lamb cutlets and also escalope of veal. She enjoys salmon on a bed of rice, and *en croute*, and she also likes steak, but for her it must be very well done – almost cremated. The chef always marks her portion with a piece of watercress so that she and the page know exactly where her helping is on the platter. As an added precaution the page also puts the spoon and fork beside her piece of steak, so there's no chance of a mistake.

One thing is certain: she will never serve messy, difficult-to-deal-with dishes like spare ribs or escargots, and for two reasons. A nervous guest could make a frightful and embarrassing mess of him or herself with an artichoke or corn on the cob, and something like frog's legs or a red-hot curry might not be appreciated by everyone. She wouldn't dream of serving offal to guests in case anyone didn't care for it.

The Queen herself doesn't like shellfish, for example clams, oysters or crab, though she does make an exception when it comes to lobster. This is a taste she gets from her mother, who adored it and ordered it at least once a week as 'a little treat'. Prawns are considered all right but are never served in the shell. As scampi is easy to eat it is often on the menu. So the food will be safe, easy to handle and unlikely to displease anyone. For vegetarians a special dish is prepared beforehand, but there is also always an abundance of vegetables to choose from, as well as salad.

There is plenty to drink, though again people are very cautious, not wanting to go over the top in the royal presence. The Queen serves a chilled white Moselle or German hock from the bottle at lunchtime – never heavy wines. Red wine is also offered in a claret jug. The Queen likes red wine but she doesn't drink it at this time of day.

Salad is served with the main course and everyone has a proper plate for this. The Queen places hers at a particular angle if she wants salad, and then the footman brings the crystal salad bowl for her to serve herself. The salads are always already dressed. The Queen doesn't like her salad tossed. A royal salad has lettuce as a base, and the rest of the ingredients arranged. She particularly likes diced beetroot and also sliced tomatoes. Grated egg salad is another favourite, and melon balls with apple and pineapple chopped up small. All of these are served on a bed of lettuce. She dislikes potato salad and mixed green salads. There are five or six mixtures that she enjoys, and these are rotated day by day.

The royals refer to plain fruit – like an apple or a pear – as dessert. Everything else is a pudding, and both are available at the 'Meet the People' lunches. Pudding is served first as a proper course. Apple flan with cream is often on the menu, as the Queen enjoys pastry dishes, but they are delicate portions. A favourite pudding is *Crêpe Suzette*. These are made in the kitchen and the chef comes upstairs to deal with the setting alight. He, too, is in charge of pouring the Grand Marnier sauce over the pancakes before two pages carry in the gently flaming finished dish.

During one such lunch, Welsh mezzo-soprano Katherine Jenkins was taught to eat fruit regally. 'After dessert, they brought a bowl of water with gauze spread over the top and some fruit,' she said afterwards. 'The Queen must have sensed that I was panicking, so quietly and without embarrassing me she showed me how to wash the fruit and dry it with the gauze. Funny, I assumed that in Buckingham Palace they might wash the fruit for you!'

Cheese follows, the English way, and then everyone troops back to the Bow Room for coffee and liqueurs. Some of the Queen's Household come through, having eaten their own lunch, just to mingle with the guests – some of whom they are probably quite eager to meet themselves. Now the Queen talks to the people with whom she hasn't managed to make contact before. Once the time gets to 2.45pm she quietly leaves, with the ever-attendant corgis pattering around her, as people murmur their thanks and bow or curtsey. Then there is dead silence, followed by an audible exhalation of breath as everyone relaxes.

Usually twice a year on the royal calendar are state visits, when the head of state from a foreign power is the guest of the Queen. They stay at either Buckingham Palace or Windsor Castle, or very occasionally at the Palace of Holyroodhouse in Edinburgh. On the Tuesday, the usual day of arrival, the head of state and most of his or her entourage are given lunch in the Bow Room at the palace or the State Dining Room at Windsor. These luncheons are rather grander than the cosy 'Meet the People' occasions. As you might expect, everything is considerably more formal.

The distinguished visitors are greeted by a member of the royal family – usually the Prince of Wales – and taken to the ceremonial welcome on Horse Guards Parade where the Queen and the Duke of Edinburgh will be waiting. After inspecting a guard of honour they travel in a carriage procession to Buckingham Palace. If the state visit is at Windsor, a popular venue so as not to disrupt the London traffic, they meet the Queen and Prince Philip in a covered dais outside Windsor and Eton Riverside railway station. The royal party then drives through the town in carriages and up the Long Walk into the castle quadrangle where the Household Cavalry and the King's Troop Royal Horse Artillery will rank past them.

At Buckingham Palace the guests are taken to the Belgian Suite where they stay for the duration of their visit. Here they get about half-an-hour to freshen up before lunch.

In the meantime as many royals as the Queen can muster, plus most of her senior household, are waiting in the 1844 Room to greet the guests. Prince Philip goes personally to collect the visiting head of state and their spouse and leads them to the pre-lunch drinks gathering. Luncheon is served in the Bow Room, which for this occasion is turned into a dining room.

The Queen leads her guests, walking ahead with the visiting president, king or queen on her right. There are usually 60 seated for lunch, as all the visitor's entourage will be invited.

Everyone is placed at round tables – six of them, ten people to a table – many of which are hosted by a member of the royal family. Language can be a problem, but most of the time the royals get by in French, which they all speak well. And there are always interpreters on hand for the Queen and other royals if French won't do. Everyone else has to muddle along as best they can; an awful lot of smiling goes on in lieu of conversations.

Even though it is an important occasion, the food served will be light. The Queen is aware that there will be a state banquet that evening and also that her guests will have a busy schedule that afternoon.

No one lingers over the meal. By 3pm the entire party is back in the 1844 Room for coffee and the exchange of official gifts take place. The presents that the Queen is given vary from lavish ones – particularly if they are from a Middle Eastern country – to something as simple as a small piece of furniture. In return the guests are invariably given a silver salver and a signed photograph of Her Majesty and Prince

Philip. Honours are also exchanged after this lunch. Some guests are given honorary knighthoods, while the Queen may be given the highest Order available in her visitor's country. And that evening, at the glittering state banquet, the Queen's guest will wear the sash of their newly acquired honour.

But these grand occasions are few and far between. The luncheon hour is not normally a time when anything much happens in royal life. When the Queen is at work, she almost always lunches alone in her private dining room on the first floor. All she eats is a main course and salad, followed by coffee, brought in by her footman. And she usually serves herself from the hot plate that is left permanently in her dining room. Fresh flowers and fruit are sent up to make the table look pretty, but she is unlikely to eat any of the fruit.

On the rare occasions when she and Prince Philip lunch on their own, the Duke chooses something brand new and different from the chef's suggestions, or something he may have sampled on his interminable dinners out. They then have what they call an 'experiment lunch'. The royals would never dream of giving guests something they had not eaten themselves, and this way they add safely to their cautious menu. If they like a new dish and it is unlikely to offend anyone, it wins a place in the menu book.

Prince Charles is not at all interested in eating at lunchtime and just toys with his food. His ideal lunch is a bit of fish and a jacket potato, or maybe just a salad, though he does enjoy ice cream. He has always preferred cold food and as a young man used to enjoy avocado with prawns, a poached egg tartlet or a small piece of salmon broken up, covered in mayonnaise and made into a mould.

He has never been one for luncheon parties, and nothing has changed. He does, however, have to host dozens of dinner parties for his various charities. If he and the Duchess of Cornwall have a formal lunch at Clarence House, it will not be a drawn-out affair. The Prince is always impatient to get on with whatever he wants to discuss, which will be done over coffee in the Garden Room. At Highgrove he entertains a great deal and uses the Orchard Room, which he had built in the grounds for this purpose. At smaller house parties friends will eat in the dining room or in the garden in the summer.

Sunday lunch for royalty is completely *en famille* and they call the style of presentation 'all in' – meaning that the meal is put in the dining room, or on the terrace if it is a hot day, and everyone helps themselves. There are no equerries or ladies-in-waiting, just them. They won't see a member of staff until they ring for coffee.

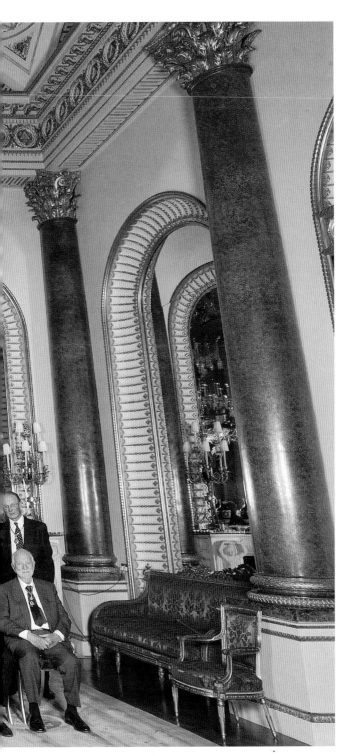

The Queen still has the full traditional Sunday lunch. At Windsor the food is not sent up from the ground-floor kitchen until the family has assembled in the Oak Drawing Room. The Queen has a pre-lunch sherry, the Duke a weak gin and tonic and Prince Andrew, if he is there, either lemon refresher or a Coke. As soon as the page sees they are all together, he sends down for the food. When it arrives, he murmurs either to Prince Philip or to the Queen that luncheon is served. The food is all waiting on a couple of hotplates on the sideboard by the windows.

They eat a small first course – usually a mousse – and then it's straight into the roast beef. Unlike in most households in Britain, where Dad always carves the roast, the chef has already done this in the kitchen. The roast – medium done, never pink – will be beautifully, thinly cut and served with roast potatoes and greens – either cabbage served in small bundles or spring greens and fresh peas. Nothing is ever frozen. They are all rather partial to an apple turnover pudding, and this is a favourite finish to the Sunday meal.

Lunch takes no more than an hour. Then they're up and straight out, to polo in the summer, or just to look at something that might be going on in Windsor Great Park, carriage driving perhaps. Unlike many of her subjects, the Queen does not have a Sunday afternoon nap!

A Royal Upbringing

THE PRINCE AND PRINCESS of Wales's close personal interest in their children, Princes William and Harry, is one of the ways in which the royal family have become more modern. For generations children were seen and not heard; they lived in the nursery, where Nanny had absolute charge.

When she became pregnant for the first time, Diana made it quite clear that she was having none of this old-fashioned nonsense; her children would not be locked away in the nursery only to appear in their party best for half-an-hour in the evening. She considered motherhood and the bonding of babies to their mother – not their nanny – of the utmost importance, and made her feelings clear to Charles. He agreed wholeheartedly and, together, they devoured books on child rearing. Diana also wanted a nanny with a more modern approach – someone who would assist, not take over – but when Charles suggested that his much-loved old nanny Mabel Anderson might fill the position, Diana was horrified. She told her husband in no uncertain terms that, sweet though Mabel might be, she was far too stiff and starchy for Diana's modern ideas.

Mabel wasn't truly stiff and starchy – she never wore a uniform – but Diana made the right decision in not employing her. It would certainly have meant a clash of temperaments since Mabel, with her years of royal training, could not have adapted to Diana's methods.

After Nanny Anderson left Buckingham Palace she worked for a short time at Gatcombe Park, the home of Princess Anne and Captain Mark Phillips. She was caring for their son, Peter, but she found the household far too informal and was unable to come to terms with the mess of boots and dogs in the hall of a royal home, and, worse, the lack of a nursery footman to help her.

Today the royal parents actually sit down to meals with their offspring, once Nanny has instilled the necessary table manners. Many years ago at Highgrove Prince Charles decided, since Nanny was off, that he and young Wills should breakfast together. Despite being strapped in a high chair, William fiddled and jiggled and managed to get food all over himself and the carpet. Charles duly sent one of his memos to the housekeeper saying: 'Experiment not a success. I think we would all get to 10am a lot happier and calmer if this was not repeated.' It never was.

Unless their parents had total confidence in their behaviour, even today the very young children would be unlikely to appear on any occasion when guests were present, with the possible exception of Sunday lunch. The royals would regard it as the height of discourtesy to inflict a badly behaved child on a guest.

When William was young the more old-fashioned staff in royal circles doubted as to whether the Prince was being given the same upbringing and taught to mind his manners in the way that other royal children had been. It was thought that his former nanny, Barbara Barnes, was a touch too indulgent with him and didn't instil enough discipline into the nursery. She was replaced in 1987 by Ruth Wallace, and then Jessie Webb who, together with assistant Olga Powell (there from the beginning), took William and Harry in hand as much as they could. Diana always had the last word and it was she who dished out the discipline, making it difficult for any nanny who worked for her to have much authority.

In the past, the nanny did all the training of little princes and princesses. When Andrew and Edward were little, Nanny was, of course, Mabel Anderson, who had already brought up Charles and Anne and thus instilled royal style into them. Prince Charles adored her, and continues to do so.

But she was still there after the long gap between the two pairs of children and ready to take over the two last-born princes. She had her problems with Prince Andrew, whom the staff politely used to describe as 'high-spirited'. In fact, the footmen were known to give young Andrew a smart backhander when no one was looking. They objected to him swinging on their coat tails.

But there has always been one holy terror in the palace nursery. Once it was Princess Anne; even earlier, it was Princess Margaret; and then Prince William. Lady Louise, the daughter of the Earl and Countess of Wessex, could also be a right little madam, but because of the troubles Sophie had conceiving and giving birth it was understandable she was a little over-protective.

In spite of – or perhaps because of – Princess Diana's keen interest in the development of her two boys, Prince William got away with more than any other royal child ever has before – particularly when his mother was about. But under Nanny's watchful eye even William went through the same routine, which starts as a game. Nanny says to the royal children: 'Come along, eat your greens, and if you're good you can press that button and a nice man will bring you in your pudding.'

One of the first things the royal children are taught to do is ring a bell. And, sure enough, in comes a nice man in scarlet livery or a black coat, and Nanny says, 'We will have the ice cream now, thank you'. And in no time at all the ice cream arrives. The children are not aware that the nice man is hovering outside anyway. But they do cotton on to the idea that, for them, help and assistance will always be on tap.

But though life for a royal child is both constricted and protected, they cannot help but grow up believing the world to be a wonderful place. Small royal children get into their parents' car and everyone outside in the street waves and smiles. It's no wonder they believe it's a friendly world. Prince Charles was allegedly quite grown up before he realised that all the warmth and affectionate interest in him was because he was different.

In some ways the royals never grow up. The entire family still love childish games like charades and hide-and-seek. Bonfire Night, known as the Fifth of November, when all British children have firework parties, is another family favourite. The bonfire and firework display used to be held in the garden of Buckingham Palace. Today, with no children left at the Queen's London residence, it is the Wessexes' home, Bagshot Park, which is the venue for the rockets, squibs and Catherine Wheels, and all the excitement of this particular cold November night that British children have felt for generations.

Nursery tea used to always be in the charge of Nanny and the children were given either milk or Ribena. Chocolate things were saved as treats, and the little princes or princesses were made to eat up their bread and butter before they were allowed any cake. Jam pennies were always a favourite – but only on Sundays. These were made with great care in the coffee room, and were actually nothing more than a jam sandwich cut into circles with a pastry cutter.

Both Charles and Diana were particular about what their children ate. Diana, a champion of additive-free foods, once discovered young William in the larder at Highgrove swigging from a bottle of pop and was horrified when she read the contents on the label. Ever since that incident, fizzy drinks were strictly rationed.

When the Queen's children were young, nursery tea was slightly earlier than for the grown-ups, so that when the children had finished eating they could be scrubbed and tidied up to meet the guests downstairs in the drawing room before being taken back to the nursery. A routine that has survived since Queen Victoria's day was for the little princes and princesses to be brought down from the nursery to the table after grown-up lunch and tea to meet the guests. When at Balmoral they were specially dressed in miniature kilts and frilled lace shirts for the occasion. Nanny escorted them downstairs and then departed. But they didn't stay long; about half-an-hour and Nanny returned for them at 6pm to take them back upstairs for their bath and supper.

The only time that Prince Andrew and Prince Edward came down to tea when they began to grow up was when they were going back to school at the beginning of term. They always came into the drawing room, where their places at the table would be laid up for what is known in the north of England and Scotland as high tea. While the other guests ate sandwiches and cakes, Andrew and Edward would be tucking into a mixed grill of lamb chops, sausages, tomatoes, mushrooms and French fries, served from a silver dish. On these occasions they were the centre of attention and greatly fussed over, as the holidays were over and the time had come for them to go back to being ordinary schoolchildren.

When they were younger, they were allowed to help bake cakes or biscuits in the kitchen. Their efforts would then be served up at nursery tea, with their initials on the biscuits so they knew which ones they had rolled out with their grubby schoolboy paws. Edward very much liked helping out; Andrew and Anne were bored to death by cooking. Charles, however, enjoyed these sessions and still likes to turn his hand to cooking – especially old-fashioned soups made from things grown in the Highgrove garden. One of his favourites is nettle soup, but he confesses he doesn't always know when to pick them to avoid being stung. When they were young Princes William and Harry spent a lot of time in the Highgrove kitchen chopping up food for their pets or making cakes with the chef. No doubt, in time, their children will find their way to the kitchen of their realm.

Old traditions live on in a royal child's life. When Christmas was at Windsor, in the nursery quarters in the Queen's Tower the children were encouraged to decorate their tree, which had been cut from the estate woods. The first thing that Prince William and Prince Harry's nanny did on their arrival at the castle was to get out the crib. Tucked away in the nursery cupboard for the rest of the year, the crib has been dressed and set up by generations of royal children. It sat on a round table in the corridor in the nursery suite. The children gathered straw from the Windsor mews and arranged the small china figures of the Virgin Mary, Joseph and the Three Wise Men into a charming Christmas tableau.

The nursery at Windsor was quite large: it needed to be, with the many young children that were in the Queen's extended family. It has four rooms, a kitchen and two bathrooms. A log fire burns in the day nursery grate, and in the morning the children listened to the guards band playing carols outside the window. As Prince Charles once remarked, there aren't too many children who have a regimental band laid on for their personal entertainment on Christmas morning.

In Queen Victoria's day the children stayed in the nursery all through Christmas, very much not seen and not heard. Until the family got too big and Christmas was moved to Sandringham each family unit stayed in its own tower – Charles and Diana were in the Queen's Tower, Princess Anne and Mark Phillips in the Augusta Tower, the Gloucesters in the York Tower, and Prince and Princess Michael of Kent in the Edward III Tower. The children stayed with their parents overnight, but were delivered to the nursery quarters for meals, accompanied by their respective nannies.

Easter, too, has its own ritual and as it is still celebrated at Windsor, the tradition survives. On Good Friday morning all the small members of the family are taken to the Home Farm. And there, each clutching a little straw basket, they search for new-laid eggs left by the free-range chickens. Their fragile finds are taken back to the castle kitchens and give to the Queen's chef to be hard-boiled. Once they have cooled, a footman takes them to the nursery, and then Nanny settles the little ones down with paints and brushes to decorate the eggs with clown faces.

The royal family have a favourite spot in the grounds, a sheltered little corner tucked under the garden wall below the East Terrace. Prince Charles particularly liked to sit there if the weather was good, perhaps because, when he was little, his nanny would leave him in this spot in his pram, a net carefully placed over the front to guard against stray cats. The royal nursery overlooks the area, and Nanny needed only to peep out of the window to check that her charge was safe and sound.

Today the only youngsters likely to spend Easter at Windsor are Louise and James, the children of the Earl and Countess of Wessex.

Tea with the Queen

IN BRITAIN, TEA – the most traditional of all meals – is served at 5pm, and it is fair to say that the royal family are nothing if not traditional! The Queen unfailingly has her cup of tea every day on the dot of five.

In the old days, tea was a courteous method of entertaining acquaintances rather than close friends. In royal circles this afternoon ritual is still regarded as a convenient way to see someone without too much fuss. Taking tea privately with the Queen constitutes a courtesy call – one that doesn't take up too much of anybody's time, leaves the decks clear for dinner and is a painless way of showing politeness to foreign royal cousins or visiting dignitaries.

Tea is, of course, more than just a drink. It can be a feast, and is enjoyed by the royal family with great ceremony in an unchanging British manner. It is at their Norfolk holiday home that they enjoy their grandest and most traditional tea parties. The Sandringham holiday takes place in the winter months. It gets dark early, so the men are forced back from the shoot as the light goes. There is no fishing, so everyone settles down in the beautiful white drawing room for tea at 5pm.

The meal has all been prepared while the guns are out in the afternoon. The Queen's staff will have set up the square card tables which every afternoon are pushed together to make a long rectangular table. Each table seats two people, and is laid up individually with Queen Alexandra's tea services on pretty pastel-coloured tablecloths with matching lace-edged tea napkins. Each place setting gets two knives – a steel-bladed one for bread and butter plus a silver-bladed one for cakes. A small fork is placed beside each plate if a gateau is being served. None of these are special knives and forks saved for use at teatime – they double duty as bread and butter knives and dessert forks at dinner.

The choice and quantity of food is enormous considering that everyone will have had lunch just a few hours before. The meal starts plainly, with thinly cut brown bread and butter, but with plenty of Cooper's jam and honey in pots to make it more interesting. Very often, looking quite out of place, a jar of homemade jam topped with a bit of greaseproof paper will be set on a very grand saucer, taking pride of place. The royal family love to buy at local sales of work, and always support any fête or garden party on their estates. They genuinely prefer the country and country things to town life, and snap up homemade preserves, cakes and biscuits. And they make a point of eating them themselves.

As well as ready-cut bread and butter, butter is served in earthenware pots for spreading on to a round farmhouse loaf that people cut for themselves. Also for spreading on bread are the various fish and meat pastes that have been potted in the royal kitchen. These are labelled and changed every day because they have a short life.

A good selection of sandwiches is available, all made with white bread and with the crusts cut off so they are soft to eat. The bread,

which is made by a local baker (bread-making in the royal kitchens stopped some years ago), is cut with a special machine like a bacon slicer so that it is very thin. The sandwich fillings are changed daily. There is always a choice of two, maybe either diced cheese and tomato or grated egg, which is very popular. Cucumber and breast of chicken are regulars. The tongue and the ham for the sandwiches are prepared in the kitchens.

Potted shrimps, still in their plastic tub but placed on a fine china saucer, are a daily delicacy. These are mainly for Prince Philip, who has a passion for them and eats them with hot, buttered brown toast most teatimes. Other guests are allowed to dip into his pot, though.

For those who are sweet-toothed there are two cakes on the already crowded tea table, placed on silver cake stands and with a silver knife at the side. It's the pastry chef's job to select the cakes that the royal family get for tea, and the result is often rather predictable. They invariably get scones, a Victoria jam and cream sponge, and a chocolate cake that also doubles up as a birthday cake when one is required. The pastry chef just makes it to the same recipe and then writes 'Happy Birthday' on the top in icing; diplomatically, one candle covers any age.

People cut slices of cake for themselves, and what is not eaten reappears the next day.

The chef will trim the remainder, cut off the dry edges and make the whole thing presentable for serving again. The royal family do not believe in wasting food.

Sometimes the chef makes little filled pastry boats with icing down the centre, and brandy snaps. These are great royal favourites. Every day he also makes tiny little scones, which are wrapped in a crisp linen napkin to keep them warm. These are eaten plain or perhaps with a little jam.

No British tea would be complete without biscuits, and the famous firm of Jacob's manufactures the selection of chocolate biscuits on offer. Jacob's also make a special small chocolate finger biscuit that the public can buy in ordinary packaging. For the Queen, however, each finger is individually wrapped in silver paper.

The royal family and their guests still change for tea; the women take off their tweeds and put on something like a pretty silk dress, while the men, after tramping the fields all day, change into a pair of flannel trousers and a favourite cashmere pullover. The room in which they eat tea is worth dressing up for. Everyone is surrounded by Her Majesty's fabulous Fabergé collection, cases and cases of it, and worth a Queen's ransom.

When Sandringham is full there are usually 14 for tea; the Queen sits at one end of the table, her lady-in-waiting at the other. There is no formal seating arrangement, so by arriving well in time it's possible to stake a claim on the seat next to Her Majesty.

She is very much in charge at teatime. In front of her is a silver kettle with an ivory handle, which sits on a stand with a paraffin burner beneath. The kettle itself tips forward to pour, and it looks like a rather dangerous arrangement. The contraption is supposed to be balanced, and as they have been using the same kettle since Queen Victoria's days and there is no family history of anyone being scalded, presumably it must be safer than it looks. In front of the Queen is a silver salver holding a Victorian silver teapot and a china milk jug and sugar bowl. Placed by these is a very long, thin piece of silver that looks like a fine trumpet. Her Majesty blows through this delicately when she wants to extinguish the burner.

She has two tea caddies at her elbow, one containing her own royal blend, and the other, Indian tea. The Queen's special blend is a mixture of China and Indian tea. Made by Twinings, it is packed in a square tin and is not exclusive to the royal family. Anyone can buy it from Fortnum and Mason.

With all the implements of the afternoon ritual set in place, the Queen herself warms the teapot – considered an absolute necessity to produce a really good cuppa. When she decides the pot is nicely warmed she pours the water she used for the job into a small basin that holds the tea strainer. A hovering page then empties this. She spoons the tea into the pot with a silver spoon, and adds boiling water from her silver kettle. It is unlikely the Queen has ever seen a teabag and she would probably not know what to do with one if she did. The Prince of Wales was once flummoxed by one when taking tea at the White House.

On the Queen's right are six cups. She serves only the top end of the table; her lady-in-waiting is going through the same tea-making ritual at the other end, with the same sort of silver kettle, and will serve those nearest to her. If there are more than usual for tea, extra cups are placed on a small table at the Queen's elbow. She pours and then passes the cups down the table, serving herself last. For some reason the men always get large breakfast cups, while the ladies are given smaller ones. Prince Philip never pours – it is considered women's work. Bowls containing sugar lumps with silver tongs are arranged along the length of the table, and there is, of course, a choice of milk or lemon.

The teapot empty, the page comes in with an electric kettle full of boiling water. This modern but necessary accoutrement is kept outside, out of sight; the page boils it as needed and replenishes the water in the Queen's silver kettle. It never seems to strike anyone as a rum way of doing things.

The Queen loves muffins, so on her left she has a shiny chrome double-sided toaster into which she pops them from a pile on a plate, handed to her by her page. In the old days they used to toast them by the fire, but not any more. Even so, it's fair to say that toasting the muffins is the only cooking the Queen ever does.

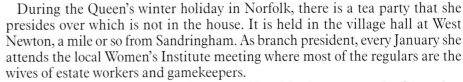

During the Queen's winter holiday in Norfolk, there is a tea party that she presides over which is not in the house. It is held in the village hall at West Newton, a mile or so from Sandringham. As branch president, every January she attends the local Women's Institute meeting where most of the regulars are the wives of estate workers and gamekeepers.

Some of these ladies come to help out at Sandringham – even the Queen has dailies. On this occasion, however, it is the Queen who looks after them, pouring tea and passing cakes to the women who may have been brushing down her stairs that morning. Yet when the Queen gets back to Sandringham House she still has her own cuppa. Her page will be waiting to brew up in her private sitting room, and as soon as he knows she is back in the house, on goes the kettle.

Teatime is rather more casual in Scotland. The royal family make their mass exodus in the summer months to Balmoral Castle, where, being so far north, it stays light very late. Tea is served in the same way, and the same ritual takes place, but at Balmoral this is the one meal at which people can be late, or even not turn up at all. There may still be shooting going on, they may have gone to the River Dee to fish, or the women might be out walking.

The Queen will be in her place at 5pm regardless, pouring for whoever turns up. She does not wait for everyone to arrive: she has her own tea, and leaves after about 20 minutes. The table and the food are left ready and waiting for about an hour, and latecomers have their tea poured by the page on duty. By then the Queen will be upstairs working on the table plan for that night's dinner, just a couple of hours away.

There is no tea at Balmoral on Sunday as the guests leave after lunch, and it is then that the Queen likes to get away from the castle if she can. Her page will order 'tea out' for her and her lady-in-waiting. The pair of them set out to one of the cottages on the royal estate. They don't tell anyone where they are going, but the page will have a pretty good idea as they will have asked for the key to one of the far-flung cottages they have chosen for the outing.

The Queen's own Land Rover is used and she drives herself. On these occasions she likes her dogs in the back and keeps a small picnic hamper by her side. As this is private land, it is one of the few places where she can enjoy driving, and she drives very well. If Prince Philip were to come with her he would insist on driving, as, like many husbands, he dislikes being driven by his wife. It is fair to say, however, that she is the safer driver.

En route, she and the lady-in-waiting will stop off to visit retired estate workers. These outings are never carefully planned, but the workers do know that at some point in the holiday the Queen will appear to see how they are getting on. Not surprisingly, most of them hang about on Sunday afternoons just in case she turns up.

Queen Victoria built these scattered cottages around the estate for times when she wanted to be alone after Prince Albert died; some say not quite alone but with her ghillie, John Brown. The cottages are fairly basic, but several weeks prior to the royal arrival the Balmoral housekeeper will have been on a tour of inspection. She makes sure that each cottage has the basic essentials – hand towels, soap, lavatory paper, candles and matches.

In the Queen's picnic basket there is always a Thermos flask full of hot water, milk in a screw-top bottle and, of course, a packet of her special tea. All the food is in plastic containers. She loves playing housewife, and in these little cottages she will prepare tea and then tidy up afterwards. China that has been slightly damaged at Balmoral is shipped to the cottages and used on such occasions. The royal family would not dream of drinking from a chipped cup, but chipped plates and saucers are considered perfectly all right for picnics.

In the days when Prince Charles was hunting he enjoyed what he called 'hunting tea'. He would miss lunch and go off with either an apple or sandwich in his pocket to munch while he was riding. He also liked to take his hip flask with him with a mixture of Gordon's gin and sloe gin to share with the other huntsmen. Etiquette is to pass the flask back and forth so everyone gets a tot.

He always came home ravenous after hunting, and today it is the same when he has been on the Birkhall estate. The staff will have a special tea all ready for him. It consists of brown bread and butter, two soft-boiled eggs, timed for his arrival, muffins toasted to within an inch of their life, homemade buttered brown scones and chocolate Bath Oliver biscuits, all washed down with China tea.

When the Queen is at Windsor Castle, tea is always in the Oak Drawing Room. This oak-panelled room with its high windows has an amazing view across to the Round Tower. It was once the King's dining room but, as it faces into the Quadrangle where the public are allowed, at a distance, the room had lost its privacy. Net curtains would definitely do the trick, but the royal family are not keen on them. Despite that, they have to suffer them at Buckingham Palace to prevent people seeing into the rooms from the high-rise buildings that have grown up around the palace. They are used at Clarence House too.

After the traditional Christmas lunch at Sandringham comes the traditional Christmas tea, with the entire royal family congregating in the Ballroom. For this occasion tea is laid up on round tables, about six to a table, and the small children join their parents.

The usual tea menu is served, except that there is also an embarrassment of Christmas cakes of all shapes and sizes sent in as festive gifts. The Queen sees most of them, and all will have been acknowledged, but the majority are then sent on to local hospitals or retirement homes. Those that the Queen keeps are not wasted; they will be served, ever diminishing, during the six-week visit. The pastry chef still makes his own royal Christmas cake, plus several for the staff dining rooms. They are traditionally decorated with white icing, snowmen and red paper trimmings – just like in many other households.

But all these tea parties are small fry compared to the annual parties at which the Queen is hostess to 8,000 people at a time. These are the famous garden parties at Buckingham Palace and Holyroodhouse, usually held in late June or early July, which most of the British public would give their eyeteeth to attend. They were started by Queen Victoria as a method of meeting her subjects. She rode among her guests, waving graciously from her carriage. Nowadays, the Queen walks and chats with people as she slowly makes her way to the royal tea tent.

Months beforehand, invitations are sent out by the Lord Chamberlain's Office to a complete cross-section of the public. Some go to the trades' people who supply the royal family with various services. Blocks of tickets are also given out to many institutions, such as embassies, high commissions, government departments and the armed services.

The gardeners will have been working hard to make sure that the camomile lawn is like a billiard table – it always is. The flowers will be in full bloom and it is a wonderful scene, whether or not the sun is shining.

A Buckingham Palace garden party is divided into three sections – the Queen's tent, the public marquee and the diplomatic tent. The Queen's tent has gold crowns on top; the public's has silver balls hanging down, while the diplomatic one is trimmed with gold spikes. At opposite ends of the lawns, two small awnings are erected to shelter the military bands that play for the occasion.

Weeks before, the order for the ton of food that will be consumed has gone out to Chester Boyd, the royal caterers. From dawn on the day the caterers will be arriving with tea urns, pots, thousands of cups and saucers, teaspoons (which sometimes end up as souvenirs), plus, of course, the food.

Outside, on the lawn, rows of tables and hundreds of chairs are laid out. All is in place by 2pm, an hour before the guests arrive. Each season the Queen will meet all the staff on duty to thank them personally for their endeavours. She then goes back inside and does not appear again until four o'clock.

Meanwhile, in her tea tent the staff will have been busy. The palace florist will have created superb arrangements, the raw materials for which will have been sent up from the glasshouses at Windsor. For a garden party, the gold tea services come out. These magnificent urns, teapots and milk jugs are laid out at intervals on long trestle tables. Gilt knives, forks and teaspoons (carefully counted) are laid in place, for tea is served buffet-style. And there is one extra treat: for those who do not like tea, iced coffee is served as well. Pages in black and footmen in scarlet tailcoats are in place now, ready to look after the guests.

Guests are allowed in from 3pm, and at 4pm on the dot the Queen, Prince Philip and other members of the royal family appear on the West Terrace. One band strikes up the National Anthem, and for the next hour the royals mingle. Each member of the royal family will takes a different 'corridor' of people, meeting pre-selected guests all along the way. With years of experience, the gentlemen ushers wearing bright buttonholes get everyone in the right place at the right moment.

Around the Queen's tent, chairs are formed in a huge semicircle for the public to sit and watch their hostess take tea. At 5pm the Queen walks past these chairs to her tent. Princess Margaret used to call it 'zoo tea': they eat while the public watch. The Queen does not sit, but stands at one end of the trestle table, usually leaning with one elbow resting on it, chatting away to either relations or retired members of her household, who are invited on these occasions. As usual in public, she wears a very bright coat and dress so everyone can see her.

In the tent, the grass will have been covered with sisal matting, and there are gilt chairs positioned around in case anyone needs one. At the entrance to the tent, at which stands the Queen's Body Guard of the Yeomen of the Guard in their scarlet tunics, a large rug is placed. It is here that, at about 5.30pm, the Queen stands while selected guests and diplomats new to London are ceremoniously presented to her.

All the while the military bands are playing tunes from popular shows and light classical music. The two bands are some distance apart, and have a very simple but effective method of communicating with each other. Each flies a flag, and when one of them finishes playing the bandmaster hauls down the standard as a signal to the opposite end that it's their turn.

Just before 6pm the Queen and her family walk back to the palace and the crowds begin to drift away. The party is over when the National Anthem is played for the second time that day. And what is the first thing Her Majesty does once back in her private apartments? She has a nice cup of tea.

A Royal Day at the Races

THERE IS PROBABLY nothing in the world that the Queen enjoys as much as a day at the races. And a day at the races with the British royal family is one of the most stylish occasions imaginable, something that all the money in the world could never replicate.

The Queen's own race meeting is held at Ascot racecourse – just a few miles from her favourite home, Windsor Castle. Years ago, those who came to the castle for Royal Ascot stayed the entire week. These days, the house party changes after two days, and there are often younger guests present: girlfriends and boyfriends of the young members of the royal family are invited to lunch and to stay for the day's racing. The change of pattern was aimed at giving the Queen a chance to expand her hospitality.

At about the same time she also made the occasion rather less formal, as a concession to changing times. White tie and tails for dinner at the castle gave way to black tie for the gentlemen. However, as both Prince Charles and the Duke of Edinburgh loathe wearing white tie, it is possible that the change was less to do with coming into the 21st century as with providing relief for princely necks.

But not much else has changed. The highlight of the day, both for the public and for the royal family, is still the processional drive down the course in open carriages, which takes place just before the racing begins.

A Royal Day at the Races

The Ascot course happens to belong to the Queen – which is another very good reason for her to take a week out of her year to put in a daily appearance there. Royalty draw in the crowds and their money; a day spent at Ascot is not cheap, and the profits go to the monarch's privy purse – her own personal source of income.

But most Royal Ascot racegoers consider it money well spent for a splendid day out. Ascot week – the third week in June – is as British as the monarchy itself and by far and away the most fashionable of any race meeting. The male punters leave behind their tweeds and trilbys and don morning suits, either grey or black with matching top hats. They wear a carnation in their buttonhole and carry a rolled black umbrella. It often rains!

The ladies have a rare chance to dress up in elegant outfits and extravagant hats. A huge hat, a jokey hat, a tiny concoction of feathers and flowers – it doesn't matter just as long as it's a hat.

The racecourse during Royal Ascot week looks like a huge wedding party. The finest thoroughbred would not stand a chance of coming anything but second to the fashion parade, and the leaders

in the style stakes, setting the sartorial pace for the other racegoers, are the royal family and their guests.

Before the racing begins and while the public are arriving and settling down to their lunch, either in the private boxes or at one of the many Ascot restaurants, the royal family will all be back at the castle getting into their own finery – the men with the help of valets, and the women assisted by dressers. By 12.45pm the Queen will be ready to meet her guests for pre-lunch drinks in the Green Drawing Room. It's quite a crowd – at least 24 people, some of whom may have just arrived for the racing and will only return to the castle after the last race to collect their cars before going home.

Luncheon in the ornate State Dining Room is a fairly brisk and simple affair, as the royal party must make their spectacular appearance in the carriages dead on time: they are never late. They sit down to lunch in their Ascot clothes, though the ladies do leave off their hats and of course the gentlemen put aside their toppers.

Everyone connected with the day has to dress up. The personal protection officers wear full Ascot rig; the ladies-in-waiting wear elegant Ascot clothes, though less grand and certainly not as colourful as those of their royal mistresses. Ladies-in-waiting are supposed to blend into the background on such occasions.

Once luncheon is over Prince Charles and the other princes get their umbrellas and top hats. Then, with their guests, they make their way to the Sovereign's Entrance where they climb into a fleet of cars for the short drive to Duke's Lane in Windsor Great Park.

At exactly 1.50pm the cars carrying the royal party draw up parallel to the required number of Ascot landaus, watched by loyal supporters and perhaps children from a local school. The first one out is the Queen and the crowd cheers.

With much smiling and waving the royal family climb into their respective carriages. A strict order of precedence is followed. The Prince of Wales usually rides in the first carriage with the Queen and the Duke of Edinburgh, while the Duchess of Cornwall follows with the Master of the Horse on the first day and possibly the Master of the Queen's Household – both part of the Windsor house party.

This is obviously a very exciting experience for first-time guests. The postillions in place, ladies' hats safely pinned against the breeze and with the footmen behind, they then drive through the park towards the course. The public bit of the day has begun.

The carriage procession enters the racecourse through what are called the Golden Gates. The royal family themselves are in the first three carriages, and the remainder contain some of the Queen's luncheon guests. The public rarely work out who they are, not recognising some minor foreign royal or a visiting statesman and his wife. The drive down the course completed, the coachmen then turn under the arch of the new grandstands and into the parade ring. Here they do a circuit of it before the footmen jump down to help the passengers dismount and the Queen, taking the lead, goes in through the glass-covered entrance to the royal box.

After the horses have been rested and watered – each carriage weighs about one and a half tons and is pulled at a spanking trot, hard work for even the strongest of horses – the carriages return empty to the Royal Mews at Windsor. The footmen who had been riding shotgun nip up the back stairs and into the royal box, where they are to spend the afternoon helping prepare tea.

The royal box, not surprisingly, occupies the prime spot at Ascot – right by the winning post. In the old days the right to wear a Royal Enclosure badge was strictly reserved for the upper classes. Divorced people were not admitted, nor indeed was anyone in trade or of dubious reputation.

Today the rules have been completely relaxed and the Royal Enclosure can become very crowded. Now anyone – well, almost anyone – can apply for a badge to the Royal Enclosure by writing to the Ascot Office.

Though many people can now get into the enclosure, the royal box itself is still strictly off-limits. Policemen, armed with a list of those who are to be admitted and given tea, closely guard it. The entrance is at the back of the stand, and inside the lobby the first thing one sees are the lifts that lead up to the first floor. This is where the viewing area of the royal box is situated and where all the action takes place.

The Queen never forgets to say 'Good afternoon' to the lady whose job it is to press the lift button for Her Majesty's guests to ride up to the first floor.

Once in the royal box, the Queen settles down to watch the racing from the front row of the viewing area, her racing glasses and race card already put in place by a member of her staff. By this time more guests will have arrived from the castle – the short way, by road. These people are mostly royal courtiers, but they could also be members of the royal family who were not in the carriage procession. They never move far away. Their task for the day is to potter around and see who is in the Royal Enclosure. They then inform the Queen if there is someone there whom she knows and who perhaps ought to be invited for tea the next day.

The Queen will say: 'Yes, ask them for tomorrow', and, the equerry concerned pops back downstairs to check if those to be invited are going to be at the races the following day and, if so, to tell them of the invitation. It's very rare for anyone to turn the Queen down. If the plan was not to be at Ascot the following day, then that plan is rapidly changed. On acceptance, the royal machine goes into action and names are added to the guest list so there will not be a problem with the policeman on the door.

Come teatime there is no table *placement* in the royal box, but unlike tea at Balmoral and Sandringham there is no question of just sitting down at the Queen's table. She decides exactly who she wishes to sit with her, and the equerry or lady-in-waiting discreetly whispers the good news to the chosen few.

These Ascot tea invites are another convenient way of entertaining as far as the Queen is concerned. By this method, she can see the third-and-fourth-tier acquaintances in her life without too much fuss being made. And if there is any minor foreign royalty at Ascot, they too can be entertained.

The hard work starts the previous Sunday, when the Yeoman of the Cellar and his staff load a lorry with sufficient wines and spirits to last the week. This haul is then driven to the racecourse and locked up overnight, ready for the start of the week's racing. On the Monday, while the Garter Service is taking place in St George's Chapel, the staff are deployed in all directions while the china and cutlery is going down to the racecourse by minibus ready for the next day. On the Tuesday itself, while some of the footmen are serving and clearing lunch at Windsor, others go down to the course with large trays of food. All of these have to be carted into the royal box and then the footmen start to lay up the tables.

By the time the Queen's coachman turns her carriage down the course, at about 2pm, her personal china and silver will be in place. Flowers from the Windsor hothouses – mostly bright red geraniums – will be decorating both the inside and outside of the royal box. The Queen's page and the Duke's page, along with the Yeoman of the Cellar – all three wearing black tailcoats – will have arrived to oversee the afternoon. The footmen will already be busy serving Pimm's No. 1 Cup or champagne. Like all British racecourses, Ascot has a drinks licence for the entire day.

A Royal Day at the Races

The new royal box – the stands were rebuilt in 2006, to the chagrin of many enclosure badge holders who preferred the original layout of the Royal Enclosure – is smaller than the old one but has far better viewing facilities and can still seat up to 50 for tea. The old box was rather like a large house furnished in Queen Anne style, with a tearoom at the back of the stand and a spacious viewing area on the other side. The Queen's viewing area has comfortable seats, carpeting and television monitors for those who would rather watch the racing with a drink in their hand.

The Queen prefers to see the real thing, and it is at these race meetings where she really lets her hair down. Her face, meant always to be impassive, shows every emotion. She can look as disappointed as anyone when her horse loses; delighted as a child when one wins. It's here that the best and the most revealing pictures of the Queen are taken.

She doesn't bet, but she does have a list of tips provided for her by her racing advisor, John Warren, and of course her own judgement of horses is astonishingly good. It probably adds to her enjoyment to have a 'pretend bet'. No one from the royal box is ever seen trotting down to the Tote; most of them have accounts with bookmakers and their bets are all placed before they leave the castle. It would be considered bad form for anyone in the Queen's party to be seen betting publicly.

Prince Philip cannot abide racing; he only goes to Ascot under protest, because the Queen expects it of him. But one will rarely see the Duke watching the racing; he spends the afternoon in front of a television set watching cricket instead. Officially he is supposed to be getting on with paperwork!

The high spots of the day for the crowds – and Ascot in Royal Ascot week is terribly crowded – is when the Queen and the other members of the royal family take the lift downstairs and out into the adjacent paddock. There, along with all the other racegoers, they inspect the horses. They do this several times a day, and at least once during the five-day meeting the Queen will walk through the crowds to the Royal Household tent situated near one of the parade rings. Here the household, ambassadors and lords lieutenant can entertain their guests and every day at least one member of the royal family holds a luncheon party in this exclusive enclosure.

The Queen knows better than anyone how much the Ascot crowds like to see her, and one of her disappointments with the new grandstands is that the royal family are now less visible. Security is always there, but it's very hard to spot.

Tea is usually served after the fourth race. If the Queen has a runner in the fifth or sixth, it is interrupted for her to get up to watch her horse run. On this occasion the Queen does not pour, as she does with her house guests, nor do people help themselves. Tea is waited by footmen. The Queen's page pours her tea, and brings her the traditional food: little sandwiches, kept in see-through plastic boxes, raspberries or strawberries and ice cream together with great blobs of fresh cream.

The tea service is beautiful plain white china with a gold band around the edges and the EIIR monogram. The soft fruit and truly delicious ice cream, made by the pastry chefs at Windsor Castle, are served in lovely Victorian pinky coral smoked glass bowls with VRI etched on them. This is the only occasion on which the Queen serves fruit and ice cream to her guests, though she loves ice cream herself.

All the leftover food is taken back to the castle at the end of the day, where it is greatly enjoyed by the staff. There would be no point in keeping it, since the Queen insists that, for Ascot week, fresh cakes and sandwiches are made every day.

Prince Charles did not immediately take to 'the sport of kings', but he changed his mind when he bought two racehorses of his own when he stopped hunting. He now enjoys watching the racing with the Duchess of Cornwall, a keen racegoer, whose first husband, Brigadier Andrew Parker Bowles, accompanies the Princess Royal to Ascot and other courses on a regular basis.

Even in the days when Charles was not too keen on racing, he always dutifully turned up to the meeting without moaning too much. Once, while he was still in the Royal Navy, he had promised that he would try to get to Ascot. He made it, but arrived so late that the royal carriages were already in procession.

It struck him that it might be fun to watch his family go past and surprise them by waving at them, then go on to Windsor Castle to change, as he was still in naval uniform. He went to the far end of the racecourse and waited for the carriages to come round. Suddenly he was aware of someone shouting at him and waving frantically.

'You can't stay there,' one of the racecourse officials roared in his direction.

'I kept saying it's only me, but he wouldn't take any notice,' the Prince said afterwards. 'But as he neared, he realised his mistake and suddenly all the shouting turned into an awful lot of bowing... I don't know why I bothered anyway,' Charles added. 'They all turned and looked the other way when they got to where I was, so nobody saw me anyway.'

As much as the Prince of Wales now likes racing, polo remains his favourite sport. Before he gave it up he used to leave well before the last race of the afternoon and make the dash to Smith's Lawn, the polo field, which is less than a ten-minute drive away. His open-topped Aston Martin would be waiting with the engine running and a small crowd of people around the car waiting to see him depart.

The rest of the family stay for the whole meeting, and around 5.30pm a large crowd begins to gather around the parade ring outside the royal box. They know it's a chance to catch another glimpse of the Queen and her party as they leave. This time the royal family return to the castle by car, but on the Wednesday the Queen will attend the annual Eton boys' tea party on Smith's Lawn and watch a polo match.

There is no knowing if either Prince William or Prince Harry will carry on the Royal Ascot tradition since neither of them has yet attended the prestigious meeting. So far it has been left to their cousins, Zara Phillips, Princess Beatrice and Princess Eugenie, to provide the young royal glamour.

Dining Royalty

IT TAKES A considerable stretch of the imagination to accept that the Queen of England enjoys a TV dinner just like the rest of us – but she does. It must be said, though, that even a TV dinner, when taken in Buckingham Palace, is still relatively formal. There's no slumping in an armchair with a tray precariously perched on one's lap. Nor is the food something straight out of the freezer, hastily rejuvenated in the microwave. The meal will be beautifully prepared by the Queen's chef, sent up from the kitchen in a large heated trolley and served by a page from silver dishes on to one of the Queen's favourite bone china dinner services.

At Buckingham Palace the television set is kept in the Queen's sitting room, and as the royal family simply never eat off their laps, they have their meals served in the Queen's dining room, but with the door through to the sitting room left open so they can watch the programme. The TV is a large flat screen with Sky+ in order to make it simple for the Queen's page to record the racing for Her Majesty to watch if she has a runner.

When dining privately at Buckingham Palace, it's always just family. In London, the Queen never has many for dinner; the group usually consists of her, the Duke and maybe Princess Anne if she is around and on her own. It is only at Buckingham Palace that the Queen ever eats without any company. At all the private royal homes she usually has either family or house guests staying, and then dinner becomes something of an occasion.

But given the opportunity to dine with each other and no one else, the Queen and the Duke are perfectly content. This long-married couple get so little time together that a meal in each other's company is still something of a treat. So when it's just them at Windsor Castle, settling for a TV dinner, the Queen and her husband sit at a table in her private dining room. They both face the TV set, which is on the magnificent sideboard placed to the right of the fireplace – one of four open fires that are still lit at the castle.

The Queen chooses the side of the table that leaves her with her back to the window; the Duke sits on her right. She likes to sit with the light behind her – not for reasons of vanity but, since she has to wear glasses, to save her eyes. The Queen is not a vain woman or else like her husband she would have taken to wearing contact lenses long ago.

At Windsor, on quiet weekends in the summer if the weather is good, they have both lunch and dinner on the East Terrace under an awning, disturbed only by the constant roar of planes going into and out of Heathrow Airport. The castle is right under the flight path, and pilots use the huge medieval building as a landmark. The noise can be appallingly intrusive, so it's no wonder the Queen and Duke don't bother with the TV set for these outdoor meals. They wouldn't be able to hear it!

Unlike the Queen, the Duke dislikes eating alone and if his wife is away he will always invite a member of his household to dine with him. But the Queen's idea of bliss is to eat alone and extremely simply. She makes herself a small jug of dry martini, leaving the ice in, and carries it through from her sitting room into the dining room.

One small course – probably lamb cutlets, with the fat trimmed off – will be waiting on a hotplate. She helps herself, and settles down to eat at the table. While she eats she reads official papers. She never bothers with wine when alone, but lets her dry martini melt down and sips at it. Her meal will be just the one course and a salad, maybe followed by an apple.

Even if alone she takes the trouble to change. On a private weekend at Windsor both she and the Duke still change for dinner, but they do not dress too smartly. The Queen will wear a short dress, the Duke a cardigan or a pullover and flannel trousers. He always showers and changes in the evening. The Queen changes her clothes but prefers to have a second bath of the day before she goes to bed.

Personal entertaining is out at Buckingham Palace, the Queen's workplace. Most of her closest friends are country people, but if they came up for an evening in the capital not one of them would dream of ringing up to beg a bed for the night. The palace has plenty of spare bedrooms, but not, the Queen feels, to house her personal friends. Buckingham Palace does not belong to her; it belongs to the nation, and the nation pays for its upkeep.

All her personal entertaining, therefore, is done in the long summer and winter holidays at Balmoral and Sandringham. At dinner she serves a completely different menu from the lunchtime one. Dinner dishes are more elaborate and richer in ingredients and sauces. The royal family never have game for lunch, for example, but for dinner parties it is almost always on the menu – providing the men have shot a sufficient amount during the week, and it's rarely that they haven't.

In a world that becomes increasingly less glamorous, dinner with the Queen at one of her private homes is a marvellous reminder of how gracious life once was. The table is always lit by candles: if it is just family, there will be four tall candles in single candleholders. The candelabra, sometimes as many as four depending on the number of diners, are brought out for larger dinner parties. Sometimes the Queen will ask for ivory candles, sometimes for red or deep pink. Each flame is protected by a small shade on a frame, which creates a warm glow and prevents the wax from smoking.

Apart from concealed strips illuminating the pictures, there is never any other light in the room. Very beautiful the dining table looks with the polished silver, crystal and porcelain gleaming in the soft candlelight.

The Queen always wears a long dress with diamond earrings and a matching necklace for formal dinners. The dress will be one that has done its duty on royal tours and has now been put into private service. Contrary to popular belief, the Queen does not wear her clothes only once or twice. They never get shabby, and they are never thrown away. There are cupboards and cupboards in Buckingham Palace where the royal wardrobe, going back over many years – and generations – is carefully stored. Naturally, all the guests are expected to dress accordingly, and dinner is a splendid sight. It is over 30 years since ladies still wore gloves at table, but etiquette decrees that tiaras and gloves are a twosome, and when it was no longer considered necessary to wear tiaras for dinner out went the gloves as well. Now the only time the Queen wears one of her splendid collection of tiaras at dinner is at a state banquet with long white gloves. Royal ladies also wear them on the night of the two ghillies' balls at Balmoral. It is not a truly formal occasion, but the Queen likes to pay her Scottish staff the compliment of dressing to the nines.

These days, wherever dinner is being served, the men wear dinner jackets and black tie, or in Scotland those who are entitled by birth wear the kilt. If the party is taking place at Windsor Castle in the State Dining Room, Prince Charles and Prince Philip wear what they call the Windsor Coat, a dinner jacket based on a hunting design, in navy blue with a red collar and cuffs, modelled on one created by George III to be worn at Windsor back in the late 18th century.

At Windsor, incidentally, the guest list is often increased when the Queen invites the officer of the guard from the barracks to attend dinner. This makes a good opportunity for the Queen and her family to meet any new guards officers who have recently joined whatever regiment is stationed near by.

Dressing for dinner was once much more formal, with the men sporting both tails and decorations. But times have changed and a dinner jacket without decorations has become acceptable, even for Royal Ascot week, which was always the grandest and most dressy private week of the year.

A lot of things changed during the terrible fuel crisis in Britain in the early Seventies. The Queen felt she had to be seen doing her bit and cutting back like her subjects. Like the rest of the British population she went without heating, sometimes doing her paperwork wearing a mink coat to keep warm!

But not a great deal changes in the royal family's routine. You could set your watch by the time they eat their meals, and the precision with which the staff ensure they arrive is a marvel. Everything is done according to tradition. They have a number of different ways even for setting a table. When the Queen is on her own the cutlery for the whole meal is put in place. If there are just two of them eating, they help themselves to food from a hotplate. The Queen's rules are that there should be more than two before she is waited on.

At formal dinners, the cutlery is put down for the first and second course and then the footmen 'crumb' – wipe down the table with a napkin on a small silver salver – before putting down the cutlery separately for the pudding or savoury and dessert. This is exactly the same procedure as in a good restaurant, whereas at lunch all the silver is put in place from the start of the meal. Butter is served individually to each guest at dinner – everyone has their own little glass dish with a couple of pats. Salt and pepper cruets are also a pair per person, put in front of each place setting. When dessert – bowls of apples, pears, peaches or grapes – is handed by the footmen, each dinner guest is given a finger bowl on a gilt dessert plate with a gilt knife, fork and spoon. These are set just to the left of the place setting. The guests then lay out their own cutlery for the fruit course.

Some of the Queen's china is very old indeed, though much of her collection consists of wedding presents from when she and Prince Philip were married in 1947. She is very interested in fine china, and every formal printed menu tells the make and pattern of the china used for each course. This gives people a chance to see the Queen's collection, but there is also another consideration. The china does make a talking point with a dull guest, and some of the Queen's duty guests can be very dull indeed.

But what about the royal food? Dinner always starts with a hot fish dish – perhaps fried scampi diced up with breadcrumbs, or a Scampi Mornay. The chef might make a rice mould and fill it with diced white fish covered in various sauces. Often, particularly at Balmoral where the river runs almost outside the front door, there will be a salmon starter – perhaps a quiche.

Another regal favourite is a celery heart wrapped in a thin slice of ham and covered with cheese sauce. Soup is hardly ever on the menu (though, surprisingly, it is served at state banquets). Only if there are children staying in the royal nursery is soup selected for supper, served in lovely little earthenware pots with lids.

The grown-ups are invariably given game. Pheasant or partridge are served virtually every night at Sandringham during the winter holiday, and grouse is almost always on the menu every night at Balmoral and frequently at Prince Charles's nearby home, Birkhall. The Prince likes to eat game as he considers it totally organic.

The royal family do not hang the birds for too long, rarely more than a couple of days. They do not like the meat to be 'high', as in so many British country homes, especially as well-hung game is an acquired taste that not all their guests might appreciate. They are also aware that there are people who do not care for game, and therefore one of the page's jobs at both Balmoral and Sandringham is to catch the guests after tea to ask if they would rather have chicken for dinner. A good many of the ladies settle for the farmyard variety bird.

While the page is doing his research, the Queen is working out the evening's seating plan, which she then passes to

him. It is his duty to mark beside each guest's name what they wish to eat, thus avoiding the 'chicken or grouse?' question once everyone is seated at table. Come dinnertime, the footmen know exactly how to follow through. They know that those who are having game are served with fried breadcrumbs, and that those who are eating chicken are to be given bread sauce, and of course they offer two gravies.

Salad, always served with dinner, is the Queen's prop. As it is not polite for anyone to be eating after she has finished, if one of her guests (and it's usually Prince Charles) is slow, she keeps a fork in her hand and toys with her salad until the moment is right to ring for the staff to come in and clear. The electrically wired bell, which she presses personally, is discreetly hidden immediately under the table at her place.

For a third course, lucky guests are served with a sweet or savoury soufflé. The Queen really likes these – either chocolate or cheese or, a special favourite, a very mild kipper soufflé. Royal soufflés rarely sink, but in case of emergencies the chef always makes an extra one to keep in reserve. Souffles can also burn, and butter-fingered footmen have been known to drop them. Sixteen for dinner means not four but five soufflés rising, hopefully on time. It is one of the few dishes that the Queen will sit and wait for. If all goes well, the staff get the spare one, and the senior staff make a beeline for the kitchen on the days when soufflés are on the menu. Why not? Souffles don't keep, so someone might as well eat them up.

There's a very strict rule – one which is, however, constantly broken – that no dish must be touched after it has left the table. If there is a piece of grouse or salmon left over it is supposed to be taken to the kitchen to be 'recycled'. However, one or two of the pages on dinner duty don't bother to go to staff supper; they know that there'll be a portion of something delicious left over. After the Queen's bell has gone for the staff to clear, a fly on the wall would see one or two of the older pages gulping down their clandestine dinners in the silver pantry while waiting for the bell to go again. Naturally they are always a course behind the royal table, and undoubtedly the royal family know exactly what is going on. Unlike Queen Victoria, they are probably rather amused.

The Queen has a sweet tooth and for family meals loves chocolate Dalmatian ice cream for pudding, served in bowls with scoops. This is plain vanilla ice cream with mint chocolate chips in it, and looks rather like a Dalmatian dog. The Queen believes she invented it, not knowing that it has been on sale for many years in the USA. Another favourite, which is also served when there are guests, is a *bombe*, meringue-covered ice cream piped with thick cream; as an added refinement the chef breaks up chocolate mints and uses them as decoration. One rule of royal style is that cheese is never served at dinner.

Dining Royally

Even today the ladies still leave the room after dinner to 'powder their noses', as going to the bathroom is euphemistically called even in royal circles. Needs of nature taken care of, they head for the drawing room (the sitting room is strictly for the Queen's private use in all her homes) where they gossip, play the piano or help themselves to surprisingly manly drinks like scotch, brandy or vodka from the tray.

While still at the table, the men pass around the Taylor's vintage port, always from the right (it is considered unlucky to ever pass the decanter anti-clockwise – an old British naval superstition). The port itself may have been presented to the family on some royal occasion years earlier and laid down in the royal cellars ever since.

Over the years the length of time before the men joined the ladies has become shorter. In Princess Diana's day it was no more than a brief formality. The Prince and Princess led much quieter social lives than the Queen and hardly entertained at all. At Highgrove the Prince employs two butlers, a footman and an orderly, a Gurkha soldier. (The Prince is Colonel-in-Chief of the Royal Gurkha Rifles.)

The Princess Royal is quite the most casual of the family and very often has her and her

husband's dinner served on a tray. They'll both sit on low stools and watch television while they eat. She rarely cooks the food herself – neither of them do much cooking at home – though they do like to fiddle about with the barbecue out-of-doors. And neither of them ever washes up.

Within reason, most of the royal family can choose to be as private as they like. The Queen is not so fortunate. There are so many people she must entertain. Nor is she always in the position of being able to pick her table companions – many of them are duty guests.

Those invited to 'Dine and Sleep' at Windsor Castle include Cabinet ministers, ex-Prime Ministers and high-ranking civil servants. During the Easter visit the Queen hosts one or two of these evenings a week.

At least eight people are invited, normally with their spouses. A problem with 'Dine and Sleeps' in this vast castle is that

guests can get lost, and one night certainly isn't long enough to get to know the way around. The Queen is aware of this and the guests, who arrive at about 6.30pm, are fetched from their quarters by a page after they have had time to freshen up and taken down to the Green Drawing Room, where drinks are served. They proceed to the State Dining Room for dinner itself, which will comprise much the same kind of food and service as at any other non-private dinner party.

What does change are the props. Windsor Castle has the finest collection of rare old Waterford glass in the world. It was all bought by George III and George IV and the glasses go off at an odd angle because each one is handmade. This glass is used at a 'Dine and Sleep' dinner party, and the footmen wear their scarlet jacket, black trousers, white tie and waistcoat. The pages wear white tie, stiff shirt and black coat, all with gold 'EIIR' buttons.

Windsor Castle also has a surprising collection of chamber pots, though of course the Queen does not show these to her guests. They are kept in a cupboard in a small mirrored passage between the State Dining Room and the Octagonal Dining Room. They were always kept between the two dining rooms, since the nearest lavatory was a considerable distance away in Queen Victoria's day. In those days of gargantuan eating and drinking, they were there for the gentlemen guests' benefit. Happily for the staff, Windsor Castle now has cloakrooms, but the dozen or so chamber pots remain. And very pretty they are too.

The best part of 'Dine and Sleep' as far as the guests are concerned is that dinner is always followed by a tour of the Royal Library. This really is a rare privilege, as it is a room full of treasures that few people ever see. The Queen herself is fascinated by all that the room contains. It holds her family history, plus a fine collection of Leonardo da Vinci drawings. The Queen is very knowledgeable about what's what in the house, so at about 10.30pm she herself shows her guests around, and is a fascinating guide. For members of the household and family, who know it all backwards, a temporary bar is set up with a vast array of drinks.

Of course, at various times throughout the totally predictable royal year the Queen is host to an official dinner – usually for around 60 people and held at Buckingham Palace. These dinners are more for politicians than for heads of state. The latter get the much grander state banquet, which is held in the Ballroom – a huge, high-ceilinged, cream-painted room with mouldings and pillars picked out in gold leaf, dominated by chandeliers and the Queen's throne, set under a vast red velvet canopy. On these occasions, all of Queen Victoria's solid gold plate is brought out for the night.

The routine for a state banquet is like a well-rehearsed play, with curtain up at 7.50pm on a spring or autumn Tuesday evening when Prince Philip leaves his and the Queen's apartments in Buckingham Palace. He runs downstairs in white tie and tails, ignoring the lift, to the Belgian Suite, where the distinguished guests are waiting.

It might be the president of somewhere as important as the USA and his first lady, or the head of state of any small foreign power. It could be foreign royalty, but no matter how rich or poor their country they are about to be treated to one of the greatest pieces of theatre that exists today, and it is all in their honour. Prince Philip escorts them to the White Drawing Room, where most of the royal family are waiting to receive the guests. Drinks are served before the family pose for official photographs. It is considerably more impressive than simply taking dinner with the Queen – an experience that even the wealthiest and the most sophisticated of statesmen will never forget.

Once the guests have been taken to the White Drawing Room they are treated to a surprise that few ever see. Suddenly a cabinet and huge mirror that dominate one corner of the white and gold room swing back. Through this secret entrance the Queen (and entourage) enters from her own apartments, glittering in tiara and priceless jewels; then the whole thing is swung back into place. The state banquet, the veritable jewel in the crown of a state visit, can now begin.

That morning, deep in the basement of the palace, strongrooms will have been opened and Queen Victoria's gold plate washed in warm soapy water by the Yeoman of the Glass and China Pantry and his staff. The table will have been set with this gold plate and crystal glasses, and candelabra will have been placed dead centre down the long tables by the smallest and lightest footman. Wearing something like airline socks on his feet, he will have made his way down the middle of the table, making sure that each candelabrum is in exactly the right place.

Just before the banquet begins, hundreds of ivory-coloured candles are lit, brilliantly illuminating the vast Ballroom. One hundred and seventy people will be seated at the U-shaped table, including high-ranking military men, church dignitaries and others with a special interest in the guest's country. Orders, miniatures and decorations are worn, and the women wear tiaras, long gloves and spectacular jewellery.

The royal family go in procession to the Ballroom, led by the Lord High Steward and the Lord Chamberlain carrying their wands of office. These two dignitaries used to walk backwards, facing the Queen and her guests, but that practice has been abolished. The Queen partners the visiting head of state, while Prince Philip leads in his or her spouse. Others follow in order of seniority.

This is an occasion when the Queen does not lead everyone in to dinner. All except the principal guests are assembled and waiting, standing by their gilt chairs. Not until she is seated do they sit. Although the Archbishop of Canterbury is usually present, grace is not said in deference to the different religions of the many nationalities gathered together.

Microphones will have been hidden in floral arrangements in front of the Queen and the visiting head of state, ready for their speeches, after which they drink to the health of each other's country. Above, in a small gallery, a regimental string orchestra plays the national anthems and then continues, more softly, through dinner – invariably soup, lamb, pudding, fruit and petits fours – which is served with military precision, facilitated by a 'traffic light' system between kitchens and banqueting room.

Two hours quickly pass, and once bagpipers have marched around the table playing Scottish tunes it is time for the Queen to lead her visitors into an adjoining room for coffee – perhaps to the relief of those by now desperate to converse with someone in their own tongue. A state dinner can be quite a strain.

A Royal Wedding

EVERYONE LOVES A WEDDING, and nothing fires the imagination of the British quite as much as a full-scale royal wedding. The day is an excuse for pageantry. Hundreds of thousands of well-wishers throng the capital to line the route of the processions on an occasion that adds a great splash of glamour to daily life and a lot of excitement.

In some ways it's more fun for us than for the couple concerned. Unfortunately they aren't allowed too much say in their wedding, because from the moment that their engagement is officially announced the royal machine takes over. Royal brides-to-be, like Lady Diana Spencer, Sarah Ferguson and Sophie Rhys-Jones, more or less had to do what they were told. It's not just their wedding, it's a national occasion. It's not just their day, it's a day for the people.

Even when Charles and Camilla married at the Guildhall in Windsor in April 2005 the subsequent service of thanksgiving in St George's Chapel was televised internationally. One of the things Camilla admitted scared her most was meeting the well-wishers allowed into the Windsor Castle precincts. It reminded her that she too was now public property.

There are many differences between a royal wedding and an ordinary one, besides the scale of the event. Traditionally it is the bride's father who pays when his daughter marries, but when one of her sons weds the Queen picks up the bill regardless. This might well be a relief to the bride's family, considering how grand the wedding has to be. The snag is that the bride is not allowed to invite too many guests to the ceremony. Her family and friends may be thin on the ground as she walks up the aisle.

The reason for this apparent injustice is that so many people are begging for invitations. The most important group of invitees are those known as the 'Magic Four Hundred'. These consist of royalty from all over the Europe who must be invited, regardless of whether they are still throned or long deposed. Not one single relative of the Queen must be left out. And, of course, there are Her Majesty's personal friends – those who make up her intimate circle.

Then there are a great many places requested by the Foreign Office 'for diplomatic reasons'. Presidents and heads of state of friendly countries are invited, along with their ambassadors. Representatives from the British government, the Church and the armed forces must also be asked, and old family retainers are invited, including some of the staff from the Queen's private homes.

At Prince Charles's first wedding, St Paul's Cathedral could have been filled four times over, but since space is always at a premium the happy couple have no choice but to accept a list largely consisting of people they have never met and will probably never meet again. Lady Diana and Sarah Ferguson didn't even have much influence on what was served at the wedding breakfast. The Queen decides the menu for the day, and she usually settles for a cold buffet of lobster, salmon, chicken and tiny lamb cutlets accompanied by various salads.

One consolation, however, is that at least the royal bride-to-be does not have to bear the burden of sending out all the gold-edged invitation cards. They are always from the Queen. Nor does she have to worry about cars and transport for everyone. The staff of the Lord Chamberlain's Office does all this.

They also arrange every detail of the venue, and this, of course, is the first of many important decisions that are made. The usual location chosen is Westminster Abbey, since it's near Buckingham Palace. Occasionally St Paul's is an alternative because the fine old Wren cathedral seats more people – as was necessary when Charles and Diana married. And of course St George's Chapel has become popular of late.

Diana Spencer was not particularly enamoured with the workings of the royal machine, and grumbled at how little say she had in her own wedding. No doubt Sarah Ferguson felt the same. But their wishes took second place to the royal arrangements – as will the wishes of the bride Prince William finally chooses.

Of course, although press speculation will be endless, as in the case of William's long-standing girlfriend, Kate Middleton, there's no great gasp of surprise in royal circles when an engagement is announced. By the time the royal family are ready to go public with the news, they are certain the newcomer will fit in. The bride- or bridegroom-to-be has already been received into the bosom of this very close-knit 'Firm', as Prince Philip refers to the royal family.

As soon as the official announcement is made, the congratulatory letters and cards begin arriving by the thousand and flowers by the van full. They pour in from all over the world. Most of the flowers are sent to care homes and hospitals. If they weren't, the palace would soon be like an oversized flower shop. There is no great interval between the engagement and the wedding since saving for a mortgage is never an issue for a royal couple. Four or five months after the engagement ring is slipped on the young lady's finger the marriage band follows.

Similarly, there are no great problems about fixing a date, though again others choose this. There is always plenty of time and warning to ensure that everything runs smoothly. All royal fixtures, including weddings, are plotted six months in advance. When a romance looks like becoming serious, long before any engagement is announced, palace officials who plan the royal routine block off a space in the royal diary in anticipation.

Spontaneity is not something the royal family ever indulge in. Though the Prince of Wales announced his engagement at the end of January, he had known for some months that he intended to propose – it must have required great strength of mind to keep it to himself. Had Lady Diana done the unthinkable and turned him down, the Prince would have had a lot of time for polo in the summer of 1981.

But she said yes, of course. The Lord Chamberlain's Office was therefore able to get on with the seating arrangements for the cathedral. These are most certainly not on a first-come first-served basis. The seating plan is a miracle of expert organisation, with every wedding guest given his or her own seat number. And there are lots of gentlemen ushers in attendance to make sure everyone is in their right place.

Colour-coded cards delineate different areas in the abbey or cathedral. This prevents the sort of embarrassing situation where a gamekeeper who arrives early is put in a front seat while a duchess who turns up later gets tucked in at the back. It's a delicate business ensuring that no one is offended.

People noticed that at Prince Charles's first wedding Nancy Reagan was placed behind the King of Tonga. Odd, they thought, but by royal reckoning if you're monarch of even the tiniest country in the world, you're more important than the wife of the President of the USA.

As a rule, at ordinary weddings everyone who goes to the church goes to the wedding breakfast. This is another tradition that is turned round at a royal wedding. The guest list for the festivities back at the palace is a small one, probably comprising no more than 40 guests: the immediate family and a select few others.

For those who might otherwise feel left out in the cold, the Queen gives a ball two nights before the wedding. As many of the 'Magic Four Hundred' as can be squeezed in are invited. The bride's side is probably allowed about a hundred places at this most glittering affair, which does at least mop up friends and family who have not managed to get invited to the wedding ceremony. But an awful lot of editing of the list is inevitable, and there are still those who cannot be included.

The Duchess of York's father, Major Ronald Ferguson, decided to give a dance for his daughter three nights before the wedding so most of her extensive circle of friends could be included in part of the celebrations, if not at the wedding itself. A large tented area in the polo ground at Smith's Lawn, Windsor, was the venue for 750 guests. Almost all the royal family were there, as was Nancy Reagan, who had flown from the USA for the wedding itself. The

Wedding Gown of The Lady Diana Spencer

Fergusons hosted the party, which consisted of a dinner for the immediate royal family first and then a dance with breakfast for Fergie and Andrew's friends. Apart from the pouring rain, the evening was a great success.

One tradition common to both ordinary and royal weddings is the stag night. But the royal variation is generally held some days before the wedding, to prevent having a hung-over bridegroom on the wedding morning. Fergie and Diana decided to intrude on Prince Andrew's stag night. They dressed themselves up as policewomen and took themselves off to Annabel's, the exclusive Mayfair nightclub, where they thought the stag night was taking place in a private room.

A couple of friends saw through the disguises, however, and they were forced to leave, after much giggling, only to accost Andrew later at the gates of Buckingham Palace. Fergie, still in her policewoman's uniform, tried to prevent him from entering.

Once the wedding is over and the new husband and wife are safely back at Buckingham Palace, the photographers wait in the Throne Room to record the event for posterity. Several balcony appearances and the photography create a convenient time gap for the other guests to get back to the palace through the packed streets.

Between 1.30pm and 2pm the favoured guests sit down behind the closed doors of the chosen reception room – usually the Ball Supper Room. The attendant footmen are always left outside, only appearing when rung for. Inside the sanctuary the royal family and their guests eat their cold buffet, make congratulatory toasts and cut the cake – with a sword – which often leads to a lot of good-natured noise and giggles.

Palace chefs make the wedding cake, but there is friendly rivalry between the catering corps of the three armed services, who each make a cake of their own. They aim to create the most attractive cake of all to outdo the culinary skills of the Queen's team. There are also a considerable number of amazingly professional-looking cakes that arrive from the public as presents. These are all put on display and eventually cut up, neatly boxed and distributed to staff and friends who weren't at the wedding.

All the arrangements have to run with split-second precision, and this means an incredibly busy time for the Queen's staff. From the moment that the announcement of the engagement is made, all staff leave is cancelled until after the wedding, but no one minds. Everyone who works at the palace wants to be involved in the action and excitement and to know exactly what's going on.

Buckingham Palace has its own very efficient grapevine, and more often than not the staff know what's happening days before the announcement is made. The staff immediately start a collection for the wedding present: first time around Prince Charles's staff bought him silver menu holders fashioned in the shape of Prince of Wales feathers. These were welcome, since no royal meal is served without menu cards.

Then comes the lull before the storm. The officials are busy dealing with the details of the wedding day, and acknowledging messages, flowers and gifts. Until the actual day dawns, the staff have comparatively little to do. But when it does come, it's all hands on deck with the normal routine out of kilter.

The palace becomes even more of a well-oiled machine, and each valuable member one of its cogs. All day people are eating snatched meals in shifts, particularly in the staff dining room, where lunch is served at half-hour intervals to accommodate those who have been on say carriage duty or at the cathedral. Thus the senior staff may have a very early lunch while the ceremony is going on, so that they are on duty for the return of the wedding party. The stablemen, on the other hand, don't get lunch until about 4pm – each horse has to have its harness taken off and be stabled, and the carriages put away. The footmen who have been riding pillion on the carriages are ready for their meal and a glass of wine or champagne to drink the royal toast.

Inevitably it is the kitchens that are the most overworked areas of the bustling palace, coping with all the preparations for and serving of the wedding breakfast, while trying at the same time to keep the rest of the palace fed at varying times. An event as major as a royal wedding necessitates the drafting in of extra staff; it would be far too much to expect the regulars to cope with all the added preparations. Once they are kitted out in their livery, much of it dating from Queen Victoria's time, no one would be able to tell the difference between them and the old hands.

Around 3.30pm the Royal Mews staff are busy again, with another carriage and horses being prepared for the newlyweds' departure. Upstairs, the honeymooners are changing into their going-away clothes, but for where? That's just what the world's press are clamouring to know, and often the venue of the first night of the honeymoon is a well-kept secret too.

Before the decommissioning of the Royal Yacht *Britannia*, the couple were usually treated to a cruise – Princess Anne and Mark Phillips went to the West Indies, for example, while Charles and Diana chose the Mediterranean and Fergie and Andrew the Azores.

Privacy is at a premium for royalty and no press boat, however persistent, was able to follow *Britannia* on her secret honeymoon routes.

Just like all marriages, royal weddings have their memories. Diana muddled the order of her husband's names during the service. Sarah repeated Andrew's name in her anxiety not to make a mistake. It was Prince William who, as one of the sailor-suited pageboys, stole the show at her wedding. Few people who watched the service will ever forget his wriggling and jiggling. He was seated next to his cousin, Laura Fellowes, and halfway through the service they began to get bored. He fiddled with the cord of his sailor hat, pushing it to the back of his head. He then tried to remove the mini-knife that formed part of his outfit. Having failed, he tried to engage Laura's attention. She refused to be distracted, so he stuck his tongue out at her.

Television crews, who had been instructed not to focus too much on the young attendants, did their best to keep the cameras on the business in hand but could not resist the occasional close-up of William's antics.

Whenever the royal family reminisce about previous weddings it is that of Princess Alexandra and Angus Ogilvy that is always mentioned, even though it was long ago in 1963. It was perhaps the nearest to a real family wedding that is possible for the royals to have, and Alexandra herself is the most popular member within the royal circle, loved by everyone. Her pre-wedding ball for 2,000 guests was held at Windsor Castle and was very grand; the royals still remember it as the best ever.

It's a family joke remembering how Prince Charles upset the make-up artist on the day of Princess Anne's first wedding. The Queen had left her own rooms and gone upstairs, as mother of the bride, to see how her daughter was. A French cosmetic artist had just finished making up the Princess's face, and Charles, who was with his mother, said: 'Oh, Anne, you've got far too much make-up on.'

'Perhaps His Highness would like some as well?' the make-up artist said brusquely. 'No thanks,' said Charles, eyebrows raised, as he fled down the corridor.

There was a time when to be royal meant marrying for duty. The Queen's grandmother, the stately Queen Mary, had originally been engaged to the Duke of Clarence. His sudden death changed the situation. But Queen Victoria was convinced that May of Teck should marry one of the royal princes. Dutifully, Mary married her dead fiancé's brother, and became Queen when he ascended the throne as King George V.

No one would be expected to make such a sacrifice today, and indeed, within reason, royalty can now marry whom they like. There would be no objections to William and Kate getting married because she is not from an aristocratic family. Indeed the fact that she is from such an ordinary, happy family background doesn't matter at all. The fact she has known William for so long and he trusts and loves her counts far more than land or titles these days. But it doesn't mean Miss Middleton won't encounter certain problems; marrying into an institution like the British monarchy is never going to be easy.

Even the Queen, who allegedly fell deeply in love with Prince Philip while just 13, had her problems. Her father, King George VI, was not certain that the British public would take a Greek prince of German descent to their hearts. The fact that Philip had fought in the Royal Navy during the war and spent much of his life in Britain did not ease the King's reluctance. It was only the young Princess's determination – with a little help from Lord Mountbatten, Prince Philip's uncle – to marry the man she loved that eventually brought into being one of the most successful royal marriages of the 20th century.

It was a wedding that took place in the aftermath of war, when Britain was deep into austerity. At first it was going to be held quietly and privately in St George's Chapel at Windsor, but then the Labour government of the day relented and permitted the marriage to become a public occasion, realising that such an event would lift the hearts of a war-weary people. And the people showed astonishing generosity when the news was announced. Women sent sugar and flour from their meagre rations to help towards the wedding cake; others sent the 21-year-old Princess Elizabeth precious nylon stockings and hoarded lengths of fabric for her gown. People even sent books of clothing coupons, but these had to be returned since it was illegal for them to be passed on.

Nothing changes. When royalty marries, in spite of their wealth and riches, gifts still pour in. There were so many at Charles and Diana's wedding that the Queen turned what was called the Trades' Door of Buckingham Palace into the Side Door, changing the name so as not to offend people who delivered presents there.

While most people use initiative and inspiration when choosing gifts that they think the royal couple concerned might like, governments seek advice. The Canadian government presented Charles and Diana with an entire bedroom suite, including wardrobes, dressing tables and a four-poster bed, all in Canadian maple. In these cases royalty aren't backward in coming forward about saying what they would like!

When Prince Edward married Sophie Rhys-Jones in 1999 it was in stark contrast to the marriages of the Queen's other three children.

For the marriage of the Prince of Wales in 1981, the armed forces were mobilised to line the route and there were street parties all over the country. The bride arrived in a glass coach accompanied by a Captain's Escort. Sophie arrived by car from Royal Lodge, where she had spent the previous night, and the bridegroom, smiling and waving to the crowds, walked casually through the castle precincts to the chapel. Accompanied by his 'supporters', the Prince of Wales and the Duke of York, he wore morning dress instead of military uniform. It was what they wanted to capture the mood of the times, but it was still not quite the family affair originally envisaged.

Most of the royal family, with the exception of Viscount Linley whose wife was about to give birth, and some of their European cousins, were bussed to the chapel for the late afternoon ceremony. Afterwards the new Earl and Countess of Wessex were driven through Windsor in an Ascot landau back to the castle and the reception. Rather than a wedding breakfast, the guests, already in evening dress, had canapés and champagne while they listened to the speeches before a buffet dinner and dancing.

Instead of a honeymoon on board the royal yacht, which by then had been decommissioned, the newlyweds spent a few days at Birkhall, on the Balmoral estate, a favourite venue for royal honeymooners, including the Prince of Wales and the Duchess of Cornwall.

As much as he might like to, it is doubtful that Prince William will get away with such a low-key royal wedding. He will be expected to present his bride to the world in as glamorous a way as possible. It is, after all, what royal weddings have historically always been about.

A Royal Night Out

WHEN THE QUEEN is attending a royal film premiere or perhaps a very rare private evening at the ballet or opera, she and her guests always eat a light snack at about 7.15pm before leaving home. The Queen and her guests congregate in all their finery upstairs in her private dining room at Buckingham Palace. The party might consist of the Duke of Edinburgh and Prince Charles and the Duchess of Cornwall, or the Earl and Countess of Wessex, and possibly Princess Alexandra, depending on the event.

For a royal 'do', the tradition is that everyone leaves from the palace in one party, though probably in several cars. The royal family, whose whole life revolves around meals, take this early supper snack to sustain them through the evening. Years of experience have taught them that royal galas have a habit of running late, and hunger pangs can set in. Once the performance is over, they head home for a real supper.

The custom is for every member of the group to start and finish the evening at Buckingham Palace.

Real supper varies; the little light snack never does. It is always a big dish of scrambled eggs on a silver salver and another of smoked salmon, both carried in by the duty footman. A light German white wine accompanies it. The egg dish is placed on a hotplate on the sideboard, the salmon nearby but away from the heat. The brown bread is already buttered and cut into triangles. Plates, napkins and forks have been placed on the sideboard. The footman then disappears, and the royal family take a plate and fork and serve themselves. They don't sit down formally, but drape themselves around the room, either on chairs or standing up and chatting.

Royal Entertaining & Style   163

They eat only a tiny amount of these pre-theatre refreshments, as they call them. No puddings follows. Then they depart for their function, returning to the palace usually around 10.30pm for the last meal of the day – a proper late supper.

This meal will be ready and laid out in the private dining room by the time they drive back through the Garden Gate. The food is deliberately cold in case the performance does go over the allotted time. They will eat chicken in aspic, or maybe lamb cutlets, salmon, mixed meats and salads, followed by fresh fruit salad. Before they arrive, the food is set out where the hotplates stand so that they can help themselves before settling down around the table.

Again the wine will be their favourite German hock, though they drink – and eat – modestly at this late hour. The Queen likes those members of the Royal Household who have been in attendance at the performance to join the supper party when they get back.

When supper is over, the Queen's family, none of them night birds, make their way downstairs, where their cars will be waiting to take them to their own residences. The Queen says 'Goodnight' from the top of her staircase, and a page or footman escorts her guests to their cars. The Night Sergeant (the duty policeman who guards the Queen's bedroom, sitting in a little cubby-hole in the corridor) is sent for, and the Queen and the Duke go to bed. So do the staff, much to their relief.

If the Prince of Wales and the Duchess of Cornwall take a group of friends to the theatre, they are invited first to Clarence House for a snack – exactly as at Buckingham Palace. The difference is in the menu. Prince Charles gives his guests a wide choice of delicious canapés: things like asparagus wrapped in brown bread, and plates of assorted little sandwiches. There is a range of drinks, already mixed and handed by the footman from a salver. If it is a very informal evening with perhaps just Camilla, she will have the canapés made to take in the car with her to eat with her guests with a drink before the performance.

When the Queen Mother was alive she had much grander after-theatre suppers and always served hot food. If she went to the theatre or a film premiere she would take about 14 guests and ask them all back to Clarence House. The dining table would be laid up while Her Majesty was at the theatre, and there was no question of her guests helping themselves. A full staff would be on duty to serve and clear.

The gatherings went on much longer than the Queen's. It was usual to sit down at about midnight at Clarence House, and people didn't leave until the early hours – the Queen Mother was not mad about going to bed. The staff might be tired out, but she was still full of beans and quite happy for the evening to go on.

Like his grandmother, the Prince of Wales is a precise party planner. His duty staff – and there are usually around 10 of them – are informed at least a week in advance of how many there will be for supper. Royal style is rarely spontaneous – everything has to be planned ahead, and an extra guest is unlikely to be unexpectedly invited.

When the royal family attend the opera or the ballet at Covent Garden the routine is totally different: they take their own supper with them. And on the nights when royalty is occupying the royal box, the people in the audience who stare up at them rarely know exactly what is going on behind the scenes.

What few people know – and can't see from the auditorium – is that behind the royal box there is a private dining room. The royal family slip through a door from the box into this tall, elegant, flower-filled room, which will easily seat a dozen for dinner. The flowers are courtesy of the Royal Opera House. In the corner of the room a fully stocked bar will have been set up, this time provided by the palace staff, as it is cheaper to bring wine and spirits from the cellars.

The royal box also contains a private lavatory and washbasin. Royal staff take fresh soap and towels from the palace when any member of the family is occupying the box.

For an opera supper everything must arrive a good two hours before the curtain rises, and it is organised in much the same way as a shooting lunch. Plates, knives and forks, table linen and so on are taken with the food itself, packed on big wooden butler trays. It is then ferried to the entrance on the Floral Street side of the Royal Opera House. Then the staff start working on the box's dining room so that by 7pm the table is laid with silver, crystal and bone china.

Two footmen do the job, and it's hard work, involving a lot of heavy carrying up and down the opera house staircases. Menus are printed and everything is done in the grand manner.

It is a marvellous experience to be taken to Covent Garden by a member of the royal family. Sometimes they make up a really big party, using the adjoining box as an overspill. Prince Charles is the family's greatest opera buff and uses the box more than anyone else. He usually has five guests accompanying him and he likes supper to coincide with the first interval.

One of his staff – usually the valet – has to find out the times of the intervals and instruct the footmen to be ready to serve the food at, say 8.10pm. The valet, usually in an adjacent box, has to keep an eye on his watch. Just before the curtain goes up again he slips quietly into the retiring room and whispers: 'Two minutes, sir,' to the Prince.

He then turns all the lights off in the royal box so that the Prince and his party can slide in without being seen.

All the food at Covent Garden is cold because it's easier to manage – particularly in the mad scramble to get through a course, served by the footmen in their day livery, before the end of the interval. The usual choice is chicken curry, a dish they all enjoy. They will have a starter – if time allows. Normally they try to eat the first and main course in the first interval, pudding and coffee in the second. If they're running late, they leave their plates on the table with food on them, go back to watch the opera and then come back and continue eating at the next opportunity. If there are only two short intervals, there's always a rush to have coffee before going back in. After curtain-up the footmen madly clear the dining room, as it must be perfect, with no trace of the meal, when the royal family come back through.

Sometimes if one of Prince Charles's favourites, like Kiri Te Kanawa or Placido Domingo, is performing, he receives them in the royal box during the second interval. They pop upstairs quickly by the backstage stairs in all their make-up and robes. These are the occasions when the wine runs out!

What is interesting is that the Queen doesn't enjoy opera and only ever goes on gala nights. Charles loves it, while Camilla is lukewarm, preferring the ballet.

It is only on special occasions that the royal family eat supper. It is not a meal to which they ever sit down in private – in other words, when they are alone. Yet astonishingly, when there are house guests at Balmoral and Sandringham, after the film has been shown they eat yet again, even though they will have had an enormous dinner. Chicken sandwiches (with no crusts) are the usual choice, left by the footmen next to the drinks trays and eaten at around midnight.

The sandwiches are arranged on a silver dish, under silver lids, and actually rarely get eaten (hardly surprising). When they are left, they are a great treat for the duty staff to have with their bedtime mugs of tea. The Queen does not mind, as sandwiches will not keep.

Things are a little different at Highgrove; they always have a light supper on Sundays, which they eat in front of the television. They go for scrambled eggs, eggs Florentine or quiches. The Prince used to like leeks from his own garden, picked by his own hand, used as a base for the eggs and the spinach, and the cheese sauce always had to be double thickness.

In the late Seventies, before Prince Charles was married, he often travelled in the company of only his valet and protection officers. It was delightfully informal by royal standards, as a former valet recalled.

'One of the pleasures of working for the Prince that I remember with great affection were the suppers that we used to have on the train from Aberdeen to Euston,' he said.

'These were a fairly regular happening when the Prince had to come back to London after a fishing trip to Scotland. When he was travelling privately we would go by ordinary train, reserving four sleepers for our own use. We never booked in our real names. The Prince always used the pseudonym 'Mr Brown'.

'The only way that the public might guess that something was up was that there were rather more railway police about than usual. And the train was cleaner and, amazingly, the heating worked. My sleeping compartment would be to one side of the Prince, next to me the two railway police with walkie-talkies that used to keep me awake all night, and on the other side of him, his own policemen occupied the fourth compartment.

'We always took packed supper. I chose the menu and Chef made up the food and packed it in a big wicker picnic basket with 'THE QUEEN' emblazoned on it in brass. Life went on with style even on the train. I even carried the Prince's pre-dinner Martini mix in a tonic bottle, with ice in a travelling Thermos bucket.

'The food was usually salmon mayonnaise, cold lamb cutlets with mint jelly, cold chicken, selections of salads and a marvellous pudding, a great favourite called Sandringham orange.

'This is made from oranges sliced very thinly with the skin on, and covered with syrup. All the food was in plastic boxes, like Tupperware, and packed along with the ordinary King's Pattern travelling silver and cruets. We had plastic plates and plastic beakers to drink from.

We used tonic bottles with screw tops for the Prince's lemon refresher. We didn't bother with wine. It was my job to set it all out, and, meant in the nicest possible way, the leftovers went to the railway police. The chef used to pack as if we'd been marooned for a week, as the Prince knew there was no buffet or restaurant car on the train. He wouldn't let anyone go hungry.

'When suppertime came, we would open the door between my compartment and the Prince's, and he'd sit on his bed while a protection officer and I sat on mine. Once I'd emptied it, we would use the hamper as a table, and the three of us would sit there enjoying our supper, while the train rattled on down to London. The Prince would have thought it silly to eat in solitary state.

'He would lock the doors of his compartment when he slept and generally everything went splendidly. Occasionally we'd get one or two guards trying to be clever, asking for his ticket, but it was my job to deal with that. The only other perk was that Harvey, the royal Labrador, was allowed to sleep in with his master and therefore spared the guard's van.

'I would pack everything away in the basket after we had eaten and then we would leave the basket in the care of the guard. A railway attendant would take it on the next train back to Scotland, which kept the baskets in Scotland where they belonged. They started going missing for a while until we worked out this system. The royal family do not care for losing things.

'We also used to picnic on long night car journeys. The Prince liked to drive and the detective and I would take it in turns with him so we all managed to eat a snack, packed by the pantry in the same big wicker picnic basket, except this time we didn't bother too much with cutlery. Bacon sandwiches were top favourite, along with the Sandringham oranges as pudding, in spite of the fact that they slopped around a bit.'

From bacon sandwiches to canapés. At one time, the Queen used to give a really grand supper, usually in November. Two thousand people, including all of London's foreign ambassadors, their wives and senior staff, were invited. Most of the high-ranking Foreign Office officials were present. The Diplomatic Corps reception still takes place, but the supper has been abandoned for canapés, and the champagne for an open bar, both on the grounds of economy.

It is still one of the most splendid nights of the year, when the Queen meets her guests in the state rooms of the palace.

The staff are in their state livery. The huge ceremonial royal standard is flying on the flagpole above the palace and the entire building is open and brilliantly lit, the vast crystal chandeliers lighting up family portraits and blazing down on the polyglot collection of partygoers.

The guests begin to arrive in their chauffeur-driven cars at about 9pm, queuing down The Mall to get in to Buckingham Palace. Many guests wear national costume, while others opt for white tie and tails, their wives in evening dress. The men of the royal family are in breeches and white tie, and wearing their decorations and orders. The Queen herself and the royal ladies dress in spectacular evening gowns and tiaras, and all wear orders, too.

The reception proper begins at about 9.30pm, when the Queen arrives in the White Drawing Room by way of huge mirrored doors. State Trumpeters from the Household Cavalry sound a fanfare to announce her presence, and the crowd parts to allow her passage.

She moves slowly along the length of the imposing Picture Gallery, and gentlemen ushers bring forward those chosen to meet her. These are mostly new arrivals to the Court of St James's, who will have been received by her in audience in the previous 12 months. She moves on through the East Gallery into the huge Ballroom, and then into the Ball Supper Room where the main bar and food are to be found.

All the time, followed by other members of the family, she is smiling, shaking hands and greeting people in English or French. Being diplomats, the guests are very proper about court etiquette and bow and curtsey as if to the manner born. The Queen will have 'gone back through', as the royal family call it, into her private apartment after about 90 minutes, but the party goes on and so do the traffic jams in The Mall.

The main function of the royal kitchen on this night of nights is to produce about 20,000 canapés, and they will have been preparing them for several days. They are handed round on silver salvers by footmen and by extra staff brought in specially. For once the chefs get a brief glimpse of what's going on. As the delicious canapés disappear down the throats of the distinguished guests, more and more are brought up from the kitchen. The chefs wheel them on trolleys to temporary hotplates behind screens in the Ball Supper Room, and the footmen go to these trays for replenishments. Some food is also left on the bars, which are set up on trestle tables covered with immaculate long white cloths.

The drinks, which are already made up, are pretty weak – not out of meanness, but to help people stay sober. The late Labour politician, George Brown, used to get magnificently smashed by dint of going back to the bar rather too often. This used to amuse the royal family, who were all extremely fond of him, and staff were instructed to watch him to make sure he didn't fall over.

The party finishes around midnight, but most people go when the Queen leaves or once their presence has been registered. The crush is so great it's truly not a comfortable party, though guests do enjoy seeing the inside of the palace. When only the last stragglers are left, the Royal Household gather in one of the state rooms with a bar to have a nightcap and unwind, talking the evening over like the rest of us would.

Royal Celebrations

UNTIL 1974 Sandringham was always the roof under which the royal family gathered for the Christmas celebrations. But as more children were born to the younger members of the family – and there are now up to 40 relatives on the guest list – the Queen's Norfolk retreat became too small to accommodate the expanding family. Only Windsor Castle, with its turrets, towers and hundreds of rooms, had sufficient space for everyone. But in 1988 everything switched back again and now Christmas is always at Sandringham and likely to remain so.

Sandringham, one of Her Majesty's two private residences, was bought for the Prince of Wales (later King Edward VII) in the 19th century for the sum of £220,000 from the revenues of the Duchy of Cornwall, the traditional source of income for Princes of Wales. It was then a very large house of 365 rooms, but the present Queen decided it was too expensive and impractical to maintain so many and ordered 91 to be demolished. The family now occupy only a small part of the main building, which has comfortable but relatively cramped accommodation.

A royal Christmas has to have space for nannies, chefs, dressers, pages, footmen, policemen and valets, to name but a few. The royal family always travel with all their home comforts, which means an enormous amount of accommodation has to be found. Sandringham, of course, has its own resident domestic staff, and when the Queen first took the court to Windsor for Christmas the move caused great disappointment to the Sandringham retainers. But since the royal family dislike change, and old royal habits die hard, Her Majesty then worked out a compromise.

She used to leave Buckingham Palace on 22 December, and by Christmas Eve aunts, uncles, cousins and offspring were settled in at Windsor Castle. On New Year's Eve the immediate royal family packed up bag and baggage and moved to Sandringham where, on New Year's Day, they had a second Christmas with turkey, plum pudding and passing the port all over again. So for royalty Christmas came not once but twice a year.

Nowadays the Queen leaves London around 18 December and heads straight for Sandringham. For several years a first class compartment on a scheduled train from King's Cross to King's Lynn has been reserved for the Queen. She finds it a more relaxing way to travel and it avoids the London traffic. Most of her staff will have gone ahead of her to Norfolk and everything will be ready for her five-week stay.

The royal family are not superstitious about Twelfth Night, and Christmas lasts right through until every nut and chocolate has been eaten, and the Christmas cards, displayed on old-fashioned wooden clothes horses, are tired and dusty.

But first things first. For royalty, just like the rest of us, it's a time for buying presents (but with rather less hassle since they don't have to trudge around crowded shops themselves). Many years ago the Queen did her Christmas shopping at Harrods. Once this amazing emporium, which then held four royal warrants, had shut up shop to the general public in the evening, the Queen would discreetly appear, enter a side door from one of her Daimler cars and set about enjoying the most marvellous shopping spree. It was a great treat for her – normally she never sees the inside of a department store – but since the late Seventies the shopping has gone to her.

About three weeks before Christmas, a gift-shop proprietor brings his wares to the palace. He arrives in a laden estate car at the side door, and with the palace staff coping with the fetching and carrying, an enormous selection of goodies – mostly items for the home – is taken to the White Drawing Room. Everything is laid out on trestle tables, priced and made ready for the Queen's inspection. She does her shopping every night after dinner and makes an unhurried selection, choosing something for each and every one of her ever-expanding family. Public shopping, of course, is not easy for any of the royals, though some manage to get away with it.

And the royal family do keep Christmas in mind all year round. Country fairs that take place in the summer are another rich source of presents for these people who have everything. Spot a royal at one of these and the chances are that they are Christmas shopping. The green wellie brigade are out in force, buying. This up-market kind of country fair was one of the few places where Prince Charles got to do a bit of shopping, but nowadays he has his own 'Highgrove' shops.

The family do of course have an enormous number of presents to buy. No one must be left out. And it's each member of the family's personal staff who sorts it all out. Pages, footmen and valets all telephone each other, asking: 'What does your one want?' Surprisingly, the choices are often pretty pedestrian. Prince Charles once bought his sister, Princess Anne, a doormat. But that was what she had asked for.

The royal family's needs are surprisingly simple: it is very rare for anyone to be given an expensive piece of jewellery, for example. This is a family that really has everything, built up over many generations as their ancestors augmented various collections. Today the list is more likely to contain place mats or calling trays (a tray with complete breakfast set for serving breakfast to guests.) The men like accessories for outdoor life – shooting socks or bits and pieces to go with the royal passion for picnics.

The Queen's shopping list is the longest, as she has all her staff to consider as well as her family, so the royal wheels are set in motion several months before Christmas. At one time staff could choose their own gift, up to a certain cash limit, but now they are requested to select something from a short list of items, usually bearing their boss's cipher, or they can opt for a gift voucher.

A few days before she goes to Norfolk, the Queen and the Duke of Edinburgh will spend the whole of one morning presenting these gifts to those who work at Buckingham Palace and nearby St James's Palace; the same happens at Windsor Castle during the final weekend of the year she is residence there.

The staff Christmas party has been dramatically scaled back for financial reasons, and now only takes place at Windsor or Buckingham Palace every two or three years. Christmas begins early when the staff receive an invitation from the Master of the Household; sent on behalf of the monarch, it commands attendance at the party, but the majority of staff will not be invited on every occasion. The Queen has a large number of people in her employ, so any royal venue would become crowded if everyone were asked, particularly as each employee is allowed to bring a guest. On the night, everyone wears formal dress and as they make their way through the state rooms the royal family speak with as many of their guests as possible. There will be a lot of familiar faces, after all, and the Queen is very good at remembering the names of her staff.

Another annual event in the Queen's crowded calendar is her pre-Christmas family luncheon, which is always held in the Bow Room. Because there is only room for Her Majesty's immediate family at Sandringham, this is the opportunity for the extended royal family to get together, catch up on each other's news and exchange gifts. It is a relaxed affair and many of them drive themselves to and from Buckingham Palace.

Around this time the Queen will have been entertained to lunch by her personal staff, all those with whom she comes into contact on a regular basis. The venue changes periodically but more recently they have used a hotel just behind the palace that has been a royal favourite for many years.

By teatime on Christmas Eve the Queen will be surrounded by her immediate family at Sandringham. As soon as the smallest members of the family arrive they start putting up some of their own Christmas decorations. Each royal or group of royals will come in their own chauffeur-driven transport. The car is usually followed by another vehicle full of brightly wrapped presents. It is the staff's task to get all these parcels into the drawing room where the present-giving takes place. There are lots of corridors at Sandringham, so there's competition to borrow trolleys from the kitchen staff on which to push the parcels from each guest's quarters through to the drawing room.

Following the Danish tradition that Queen Alexandra brought to England, the royal family exchange presents on Christmas Eve. In the glow from hundreds of lights on a 20-foot Christmas tree, felled in the Sandringham woods and topped with a huge silver star, the royals gather behind closed doors to see what Santa has brought them. All the parcels are placed down the left-hand side of the room on tables covered with snowy-white linen cloths. The Queen's gifts are placed first, then Prince Charles's and Camilla's: everything is laid out in order of precedence. The children's presents are put separately around the foot of the tree.

The gifts are opened with much tearing of wrapping paper, and the same squeals of delight as in any other family can be heard. The only difference is that the royals don't have to clear up the discarded wrappings and string. The staff do that discreetly and quietly after everyone has gone into dinner.

The world received a fascinating glimpse of how the royal family relate to each other when, after she had left royal service, a housemaid produced for publication a collection of the gift tags with which the royal family had labelled their individual gifts. No doubt the Queen was not amused to see her labels printed in the *Sunday Express*, but we did learn that within the confines of the family Princess Alexandra is known as The Pud, or Puddy; Prince Michael of Kent is Maou; Lord Nicholas Windsor, younger son of the Duke and Duchess of Kent, is Pooh; and Lady Gabriella Windsor, daughter of Prince and Princess Michael of Kent, is Phub. The Queen's children call her Mummy; to her son-in-law and daughter-in-law she is Ma'am. The Queen signs her gifts from Lilibet, her pet name.

The real reason for Christmas is not forgotten. The Queen and most of her family go to church twice on Christmas morning. And while royalty prays, the chefs are hard at work in the kitchens, where they have been since dawn.

They cook at least 24 turkeys for five separate meal sittings. The junior staff are served first, at 11.30am, at tables decorated with crackers, novelties and all the traditional trimmings. Then they go back to their duties and the senior staff sit down at midday. At 12.45pm it's time for the nursery lunch for any small royals, which gives their parents time to see their offspring before they go to their own lunch half an hour later.

The head chef joins the royal family in the dining room, where he carves the turkey with style and ceremony. Apart from the moment when the Queen hands him his Christmas present, this is the only time in the year when he will see his employer. The junior staff wait at table, and, having had their own lunch, they might be a little merry. Each man will have had a large whisky or gin, and the women a glass of port. Everyone will also have been given a glass of wine with his or her turkey, but if the merriment shows, as it sometimes does, the Queen turns a blind eye.

The dining room where the Queen eats is not decorated with streamers or balloons, but is beautifully and tastefully Christmas-like with banks of superb poinsettia and cyclamen from the royal nurseries. This is the only time of the year where there are chocolates on the table, along with the sugar-coated almonds that the Queen loves. There are crackers to pull, but though the younger members of her family may don paper hats, the Queen does not.

The staff get tomato soup as a starter, the Queen and her guests a lobster dish. From then on the royal lunch is the same as our lunch – turkey, chipolata sausages, two veg and roast potatoes for all, followed, of course, by the chef's plum pudding. And it has to be over by 3pm so that everyone can watch the Queen's speech on television. Only then do the remaining kitchen staff get to eat their Christmas lunch.

Very sensibly, everyone takes a walk after lunch – if only to make room for the next meal. Tea is served with an enormous iced cake that has been made weeks before by the pastry chef. It's probably a relief that afterwards there is a little 'free time' for those who want to snooze, take a bath or play board games.

By 8.15pm everyone is eating yet again – a candlelit meal, usually of lamb. Elsewhere, the staff are given cold meats traditionally presented around a magnificent glazed and decidedly bad-tempered-looking boar's head.

Boxing Day is devoted to shooting – unless, of course, it falls on a Sunday. With Prince Philip in charge, the men are out with the dogs for a typical shooting day. It's a break for the staff who have their own parties until they have to be back on duty when the royal family return, ravenous, as dusk falls.

The royals are consistent in their enjoyment of all things traditional. Their Christmas, though grander, compares with the Christmas enjoyed by most of their subjects. And so, indeed, does Easter at Windsor Castle, with the routine not varying by a hair's breadth from that of last year, the year before or ten years before that.

At 9.30am breakfast will be served and Prince Philip will preside over a table surrounded by as many of his children and grandchildren as are available. The royals' traditional free-range Easter boiled egg is served with fresh bread, butter and honey. And after breakfast there will be a little exchange of Easter gifts, though never anything particularly expensive. Usually they give small pretty presents like hand-painted bone china boxes with hinged lids. The chef makes hot cross buns and the family goes to St George's Chapel on Easter Day, but unlike at Christmas there is no set time for them to gather.

The Queen will travel to Windsor immediately after she has completed the annual ceremony of the presentation of Maundy Money. Those who decide to join her for Easter drift in when they feel so inclined, usually some time on Good Friday, but it is not obligatory to do so. The gathering is not as large as it used to be, but the Princess Royal and her husband Tim Laurence, and the Earl and Countess of Wessex, are annual attendees.

In the normal way, over the four days of Easter all meals are served in the Queen's private dining room. This sounds as if it might be small and intimate, but it is not. Situated on the first floor of the Queen's Tower, it overlooks the East Terrace. The walls are covered in a gold damask that sets off a fine collection of military paintings. The ceilings are high and ornate, and the windows look out over the golf course, with Heathrow Airport and west London in the distance.

It is during the Easter court that the Queen celebrates her actual birthday, 21 April. She will either be at Windsor or Wood Farm, a relatively small house on the Sandringham estate a few miles from the main residence. The Queen likes to stay here for several days, inspecting her stud farm and the new foals born in the spring. Those who know her well say that this off-duty period is probably the happiest in her ever-changing year.

PICTURE INDEX

Page 34
PA.5738200: Prince Harry eats a breakfast of biscuits mixed with jam and butter in the desert in Helmand province, southern Afghanistan. 19 February 2008. John Stillwell/PA Archive/Press Association Images.

Page 35
PA.1777557: The Prince of Wales during his visit to the Nanhoron Arms Hotel in Nefyn, Gwynedd, North Wales. 30 July 2003. Martin Rickett/PA Archive/Press Association Images.

Page 36
PA.9415308: The dining room aboard the biofuel-powered royal train that will take Prince Charles on a tour of Britain to promote START, his sustainable living initiative. 6 September 2010. Danny Lawson/PA Wire/Press Association Images.

Page 37
PA.9415291: The kitchen aboard the biofuel-powered royal train that will take Prince Charles on a tour of Britain to promote START, his sustainable living initiative. 6 September 2010. Danny Lawson/PA Wire/Press Association Images.

CHAPTER 3
Page 38
PA.1063449: Balmoral Castle in autumn. 22 October 1997. Chris Bacon/PA Archive/Press Association Images.

Page 40
PA.9411985: The Queen greets David Johnston, Canadian Governor-General Designate, at the start of his visit to Balmoral. 4 September 2010. Danny Lawson/PA Wire.

Page 41
PA.8682742: Queen Elizabeth II with U.S. President Eisenhower in the grounds of Balmoral Castle. Also pictured are Prince Philip, Princess Anne and Prince Charles. 29 August 1959. AP Photo.

PA.2567571: Queen Elizabeth II talks to the Governor-General Designate of Canada Michaelle Jean and her daughter Mlle Marie-Eden Lafond at Balmoral Castle. 6 September 2005. David Cheskin/ WPA Rota/PA.

PA.3749484: The Massed Pipes and Drums perform at the 'Truly Scottish' evening concert in the grounds of Balmoral Castle. 30 June 2006. Danny Lawson/PA.

Page 42
PA.4289777: The Prince of Wales, known as the Duke of Rothesay in Scotland, with Camilla Parker Bowles at Birkhall in January 2005 prior to them leaving for a Sunday church service. AP Photo/Clarence House.

Page 43
PA.3892340: The Massed Pipes and Drums and the Band of the Royal Regiment of Scotland play for Queen Elizabeth II at Balmoral Castle, Aberdeenshire. 20 August 2006. Toby Williams/PA.

Page 44
PA.1240789: The Prince of Wales (later Duke of Windsor) and Prince Albert (later King George VI) wearing kilts during a practice shooting session in the grounds of Balmoral, Scotland. *Circa* 1906. PA/PA Archive/Press Association Images.

PA.1240784: The Prince Edward (later Duke of Windsor) photographed at Balmoral on the morning his succession to the title Prince of Wales was announced. 1910. PA/PA Archive/Press Association Images.

PA.4550062: A herd of wild deer in the hills near Braemar, Scotland. 7 April 2007. David Cheskin/PA Wire.

Page 45
PA.1060252: The Prince and Princess of Wales pose for photographers near the banks of the River Dee during their Balmoral honeymoon. 19 August 1981. PA/PA Archive/Press Association Images.

Page 46
PA.8088555: A police officer stands at the gates to Sandringham House on the royal estate in Norfolk. 2 December 2009. Chris Radburn/PA Wire.

Page 47
PA.8670907: Queen Elizabeth II and the Duke of Edinburgh pose in the grounds of Sandringham House on 4 February 1982 ahead of the 30th anniversary of Her Majesty's accession to the throne. AP Photo/Pool.

Page 49
PA.1340314: A view across the lake and gardens towards Sandringham House, a royal residence since 1861. 1 June 1978. PA/PA Archive/Press Association Images.

Page 50
PA.1668551: The Duke of Edinburgh during a clay pigeon shooting competition on the Sandringham estate, organised by the British Association of Shooting and Conservation. 23 December 2002. Andrew Parsons/PA Archive/Press Association Images.

Page 51
PA.1381459: Prince Edward shooting at Sandringham, where the royal family spend Christmas and the New Year. 3 January 1981. PA/PA Archive/Press Association Images.

Page 52
PA.1419883: The Queen rides with a groom in the Home Park at Windsor on her 75th birthday. 21 April 2001. Tim Ockenden/PA Archive/Press Association Images.

Page 53
PA.1159501: The Queen with United States President Ronald Reagan at the start of their hour-long ride in the Home Park, Windsor. 8 June 1982. PA/PA Archive/Press Association Images.

Page 73
PA.1132238: The royal family at Buckingham Palace on the Queen and Prince Philip's Silver Wedding anniversary. 20 November 1972. PA News/PA Archive/Press Association Images.

Page 74
PA.1134729: The Prince and Princess of Wales with Prince William after his christening at Buckingham Palace. 4 August 1982. PA News/PA Archive/Press Association Images.

Page 75
PA.5827849: The Prince and Princess of Wales with Prince William during a photo session at Kensington Palace. 22 December 1982. PA/PA Archive/Press Association Images.

Page 76
PA.1309368: The Prince and Princess of Wales hold a photocall for their son, Prince William, a week before he was 18 months old. 14 December 1983. PA/PA Archive/Press Association Images.

PA.1134728: Prince William waves to the crowd as he leaves the Lindo Wing of St Mary's Hospital, Paddington, with his nanny Barbara Barnes after visiting his mother the Princess of Wales and his newborn baby brother Prince Harry. 16 September 1984. PA News/PA Archive/Press Association Images.

Page 77
PA.3386476: The Prince and Princess of Wales pose for a family portrait with sons William and Harry at Kensington Palace. 6 October 1984. AP/AP/Press Association Images.

Page 78
PA.1132240: The Princess of Wales carries baby Harry as the royal family set sail for the Western Isles. 7 August 1985. PA/PA Archive/Press Association Images.

PA.4560418: The Prince and Princess of Wales are reunited with their children aboard the Royal Yacht *Britannia* after a 17-day separation during the couple's official tour of Italy. 5 May 1985. Ron Bell/PA Archive/Press Association Images.

PA.1618592: Prince Harry arrives at his nursery school in west London and gives a royal welcome to photographers. 9 December 1987. PA/PA Archive/Press Association Images.

Page 79
PA.1132166: The Prince and Princess of Wales and big brother Prince William say goodbye to Prince Harry, who shakes his new headmistress, Mrs Jane Mynors, by the hand before starting his first day at school. 16 September 1987. PA/PA Archive/Press Association Images.

PA.1159492: Prince William and brother Harry with the family dog during a polo all-star charity match at Cirencester, Gloucestershire, in which their father the Prince of Wales was taking part. 6 June 1987. PA/PA Archive/Press Association Images.

PA.1137754: Prince Harry, aged five, joins his brother Prince William, seven, on his first day at Wetherby School in Notting Hill, west London. The young princes are pictured with their mother and the school headmistress, Frederika Blair-Turner. 15 September 1989. Ron Bell/PA Archive/Press Association Images.

Page 80
PA.1129675: The Prince and Princess of Wales with William and Harry prepare for a cycling trip in Tresco during their holiday in the Scilly Isles. 1 June 1989. PA/PA Archive/Press Association Images.

Page 81
PA.1129944: The Prince of Wales holds a 'get well' balloon, watched by Prince Harry. The balloon was given to Charles by Jeanette Wilson, one of several young entrepreneurs attending a Prince's Youth Business Trust event at Highgrove, Gloucestershire. 23 July 1990. Martin Keene/PA Archive/Press Association Images.

PA.1137858: Prince William and Prince Harry meet Father Christmas – Susan Townsend from Norfolk – aboard a horse-drawn sleigh backstage at Olympia during a visit with their mother to the 1990 International Showjumping Championships. 17 December 1990. Martin Keene/PA Archive/Press Association Images.

Page 82
PA.1058711: The Princess of Wales rides a chair lift up the Kriegerhorn with Princes William and Harry, Lech, Austria. 10 April 1991. Martin Keene/PA Archive/Press Association Images.

Page 83
PA.1619003: Prince William, aged nine, and his younger brother, Prince Harry, seven, wear baseball-style caps given to them by the crew of the Canadian frigate *HMCS Ottawa* after they toured the ship, moored alongside the Royal Yacht *Britannia* on the Toronto waterfront. 23 October 1991. Martin Keene/PA Archive/Press Association Images.

PA.1138438: The Princess of Wales hugs Prince William after boarding the Royal Yacht *Britannia* with the Prince of Wales. The royal couple had earlier flown in to Toronto at the start of a seven-day visit to Canada; William and Harry arrived the previous day. 23 October 1991. Martin Keene/PA Archive/Press Association Images.

Page 84
PA.5978145: Highgrove House, near Tetbury, Gloucestershire, purchased by the Duchy of Cornwall in 1980 and now home to the Prince of Wales and his family. 23 May 2008. Barry Batchelor/PA Wire.

Page 85
PA.1055614: The Prince of Wales and sons William and Harry pose for photographers above the Falls of Muick during their traditional Balmoral summer holiday. 16 August 1997. Fiona Hanson/PA Archive/Press Association Images.

The Earl and Countess of Wessex, with their children Lady Louise Windsor and Viscount Severn, visit the funfair at the Royal Windsor Horse Show. 16 May 2009. Picture: Joe Little.

PA.6073918: The Queen watches as her horse Free Agent, ridden by Richard Hughes, wins the Chesham Stakes at Ascot racecourse, Berkshire. 21 June 2008. Steve Parsons/PA Wire.

Page 114
PA.7451522: Queen Elizabeth II at Ascot racecourse, Berkshire. 16 June 2009. Steve Parsons/PA Archive/Press Association Images.

PA.7451357: Princess Anne and comedian Ronnie Corbett share a joke at Ascot racecourse, Berkshire. 16 June 2009. Steve Parsons/PA Archive/Press Association Images.

PA.6058521: Zara Phillips leaves the parade ring at Ascot racecourse, Berkshire. 18 June 2008. Steve Parsons/PA Wire.

PA.7461376: Princesses Eugenie and Beatrice during Ladies' Day at Ascot racecourse, Berkshire. 18 June 2009. Steve Parsons/PA Archive/Press Association Images.

Page 115
PA.7456472: The Duchess of Cornwall arrives by carriage in the parade ring on the second day of the Royal Ascot meeting. 17 June 2009. AP Photo/Alastair Grant.

Page 116
PA.4771702: Miss Zara Phillips, daughter of the Princess Royal, watches horses in the parade ring on Ladies' Day at Royal Ascot. 21 June 2007. AP Photo/Alastair Grant.

Page 117
PA.7461100: Jockey Frankie Dettori celebrates winning the Ribblesdale Stakes during Ladies' Day at Ascot racecourse. 18 June 2009. Steve Parsons/PA Archive/Press Association Images.

Page 118
PA.6073800: Free Agent, owned by the Queen and ridden by Richard Hughes, wins the Chesham Stakes on the final day of Royal Ascot. 21 June 2008. Steve Parsons/PA Archive/Press Association Images.

Page 119
PA.7466119: Queen Elizabeth II congratulates her jockey, Richard Hughes, after winning the Chesham Stakes on the final day of Royal Ascot. 21 June 2008. Steve Parsons/PA Archive/Press Association Images.

CHAPTER 8
Page 120
PA.6170422: A member of staff inspects a wine glass on a mock-up of the state banquet table in the ballroom at Buckingham Palace ahead of the annual summer opening of the royal residence. 25 July 2008. Dominic Lipinski/PA Wire.

Page 122
PA.1148161: Kitchen staff at Windsor Castle prepare for a banquet given by the Queen in honour of a state visit by the President of Germany, Roman Herzog. 1 December 1998. John Stillwell/PA Archive/Press Association Images.

PA.6170287: A porcelain plate is prepared for display. For the first time ever, summer visitors to Buckingham Palace are able to view how the room is set up for a state banquet. 25 July 2008. AP Photo/Kirsty Wigglesworth.

Page 123
PA.7969848: The table is prepared for a banquet at Windsor Castle to mark the state visit of President Pratibha Patil of India. 27 October 2009. Chris Jackson/PA Wire.

Page 124
PA.5807772: The Queen gives a speech standing next to French President Nicolas Sarkozy at the start of a state banquet at Windsor Castle. 26 March 2008. Matt Dunham/PA Wire.

Page 125
PA.5807840: Queen Elizabeth II, French President Nicolas Sarkozy, French first lady Carla Bruni-Sarkozy and Prince Philip arrive for the state banquet at Windsor Castle. 26 March 2008. AP Photo/ Eric Feferberg/Pool.

Page 126
PA.5807745 The Queen sits beside President Nicolas Sarkozy for the state banquet at Windsor Castle. 26 March 2008. AP Photo/Matt Dunham/Pool.

Page 127
PA.7969826: Indian President Pratibha Patil, Queen Elizabeth II, Prince Philip and Dr Devisingh Ramsingh Shekhawat before a state banquet at Windsor Castle. 27 October 2009. AP Photo/ Chris Jackson/Pool.

Page 129
PA.7969818: The scene is set for the Indian state banquet at Windsor Castle. 27 October 2009. AP Photo/Chris Jackson/Pool.

Page 130
PA.6169501: A table at the state banquet, part of the summer opening exhibition at Buckingham Palace. The Ballroom has been arranged so that visitors can experience a real state banquet. 24 July 2008. Fiona Hanson/PA Wire.

Page 131
PA.6170425: Staff lay the state banquet table in the Ballroom at Buckingham Palace. 25 July 2008. Dominic Lipinski/PA Wire.

Page 132
PA.6170415: The Ballroom at Buckingham Palace as preparations for the summer opening are completed. 25 July 2008. Dominic Lipinski/PA Wire.

Page 133
PA.6169498: The Queen, accompanied by the Director of the Royal Collection, Sir Hugh Roberts, views the exhibition at Buckingham Palace before it opens to the public. 24 July 2008. Fiona Hanson/PA Wire.

Page 134
PA.8463314: Queen Elizabeth II and President Jacob Zuma during a toast at the start of the banquet at Buckingham Palace during the state visit of the South African president. 3 March 2010. Lewis Whyld/PA Wire.

PA.1196208: The just married Duke and Duchess of York wave as they board their jet at Heathrow Airport carrying them to the Azores for their honeymoon. 23 July 1986. PA/PA Archive/Press Association Images.

Page 154
PA.1199747: Prince Edward and his brothers the Prince of Wales and the Duke of York walk through Windsor Castle to St George's Chapel where Edward is to marry Sophie Rhys-Jones. By tradition, royal bridegrooms have two supporters, rather than one best man. 19 June 1999. Phil Noble/PA Archive/Press Association Images.

Page 155
PA.1199814: The scene outside St George's Chapel in Windsor Castle where Prince Edward married Sophie Rhys-Jones. The royal couple can be seen with their pageboys and bridesmaids on the steps of the chapel. 19 June 1999. PA/PA Archive/Press Association Images.

PA.1199777: The Earl and Countess of Wessex with her pageboys and bridesmaids (*from left*) Felix Sowerbutts, Harry Warburton, Camilla Hadden and Olivia Taylor, leave St George's Chapel in Windsor after their wedding. 19 June 1999. John Stillwell/PA Archive/Press Association Images.

PA.1199788: The Queen laughs as she leaves St George's Chapel after the wedding of Prince Edward and Sophie Rhys-Jones. 19 June 1999. PA/PA Archive/Press Association Images.

Page 156
PA.2353786: Flowers are arranged in the Waterloo Chamber at Windsor Castle in preparation for the reception following the wedding of Prince Charles and Camilla Parker Bowles. 8 April 2005. AP Photo/Kirsty Wigglesworth/Pool.

Page 157
PA.2366225: Flowers are arranged in St George's Hall at Windsor Castle in preparation for the reception following the wedding of Prince Charles and Camilla Parker Bowles. 8 April 2005. AP Photo/Kirsty Wigglesworth/Pool.

PA.2323357: Flowers are arranged in the Grand Reception Room at Windsor Castle. 8 April 2005. AP Photo/Kirsty Wigglesworth/Pool.

PA.2323361: Thousands of daffodils are arranged on the Grand Staircase at Windsor Castle. 8 April 2005. AP Photo/Kirsty Wigglesworth/Pool.

Page 158
PA.2323791: The Prince of Wales and the Duchess of Cornwall arrive for their Service of Prayer and Dedication in St George's Chapel. 9 April 2005. Chris Ison/PA Archive/Press Association Images.

Page 159
PA.2324971: An official photograph of the Prince of Wales and the Duchess of Cornwall, with their families in the White Drawing Room at Windsor Castle. *Left to right, back row*: Prince Harry, Prince William, Tom and Laura Parker Bowles. *Left to right, front row*: the Duke of Edinburgh, the Queen and Camilla's father, Major Bruce Shand. 9 April 2005. Hugo Burnand/Clarence House/PA Archive/Press Association Images.

Page 160
PA.5957071: Peter Phillips, eldest grandson of the Queen and Prince Philip, and Canadian-born Autumn Kelly leave St George's Chapel in Windsor after their marriage ceremony. 17 May 2008. Ian McIlgorm/PA Archive/Press Association Images.

Page 161
PA.5957944: A wedding group at Frogmore House, Home Park, Windsor. *Seated left to right*: The Duke of Edinburgh, Queen Elizabeth II, Mrs Ivy Kelly, Mrs Edith McCarthy. *Standing left to right*: Captain Mark Phillips, The Princess Royal, Mr Peter Phillips, Mrs Peter Phillips, Mrs Kitty Kelly, Mr Brian Kelly. 17 May 2008. Sir Geoffrey Shakerley/PA Archive/Press Association Images.

CHAPTER 10
Page 162
PA.6548611: The Prince of Wales meets dancers backstage at the Wimbledon Theatre, southwest London, after a charity performance in aid of the Prince's Trust, one of a number of events to celebrate his 60th birthday two days later. 12 November 2008. Alastair Grant/WPA Rota/PA Wire.

Page 164
PA.5104652: Opera singer Luciano Pavarotti kisses Queen Elizabeth the Queen Mother's hand following a gala performance of *L'elisir d'amore* at the Royal Opera House in London. 21 March 1990. AP Photo/Adam Butler, Pool.

Page 165
PA.7507521: Queen Elizabeth II and her party in the royal box at Covent Garden for the first performance of the opera *Gloriana*, dedicated to her. On the right are the Queen Mother and the Duke of Edinburgh. On the other side of the Queen are Princess Margaret, and Crown Prince Olav and Crown Princess Märtha of Norway. The opera, by Benjamin Britten, was composed for the coronation and celebrates the triumphs of Queen Elizabeth I. 8 June 1953. AP/Press Association Images.

Page 166
PA.1329459: The Queen Mother and the Queen are greeted by the audience at the Royal Opera House on the occasion of the Queen Mother's 100th birthday prior to a performance by the Kirov Ballet. 4 August 2000. Fiona Hanson/PA Archive/Press Association Images.

Page 167
PA.1329469: The Queen Mother celebrates her 100th birthday at the ballet, joined in the royal box by her daughters Elizabeth and Margaret. 4 August 2000. Fiona Hanson/PA Archive/Press Association Images.

Page 168
PA.1466851: The exterior of the Royal Opera House in London's Covent Garden. 17 August 2001. Peter Jordan/PA Archive/Press Association Images.

Page 182
PA.4210439: Cleaning ladies stand beside a Christmas display of Victorian silver on the dining table in the Waterloo Chamber at Windsor Castle. The centrepiece of the arrangement is a dinner service reassembled for the first time in over 50 years. Made in 1862 by the firm of royal goldsmiths, Garrard & Co., it includes silver statuettes of Queen Victoria, Britannia, King Arthur and St George, candelabra, grand tureens and dessert stands. 7 December 2006. AP Photo/Matt Dunham/Press Association Images.

Page 183
PA.4210435: Cleaning lady Sheila Tinson poses for photographers beside a Christmas display of Victorian silver on the dining table in the Waterloo Chamber at Windsor Castle. 7 December 2006. AP Photo/Matt Dunham/Press Association Images.

PA.4211747: A Christmas tree adorned with miniature crowns is displayed in St George's Hall at Windsor Castle. 7 December 2006. AP Photo/Matt Dunham/Press Association Images.

Page 184
PA.6681690: The Duchess of Cornwall receives staff and children from LATCH, the Welsh children's cancer charity, at a Christmas reception in the Orchard Room at Highgrove House, Tetbury, Gloucestershire. 22 December 2008. Arthur Edwards/The Sun/PA Wire.

Page 185
PA.8113536: The Duchess of Cornwall decorates the Christmas tree at Clarence House with Drew Turner from the Starlight Children's Foundation. 9 December 2009. Kirsty Wigglesworth/PA Wire.

Page 186
PA.8157469: Younger members of the royal family attend the Christmas morning service at St Mary Magdalene Church. *From left*: Autumn Phillips, Prince William, Peter Phillips, Viscountess Linley, Zara Phillips, Princess Eugene, Princess Beatrice and Prince Harry. 25 December 2009. Alastair Grant/AP/Press Association Images.

PA.8157422: The Queen receives flowers after attending a Christmas morning service at St Mary Magdalene Church on the royal estate at Sandringham in Norfolk. 25 December 2009. Chris Radburn/PA Wire.

Page 187
PA.8151236: The Duchess of Cornwall throws a snowball after attending a tea party for children from Ty Hafan hospice in Wales at Highgrove House in Gloucestershire. The duchess is holding a Christmas card made by seven-year-old Rhys Boggis. 21 December 2009. Kirsty Wigglesworth/PA Wire.

Page 188
PA.2742375: Buckingham Palace is lit up with the Union Flag, highlighted by snowflakes and wrapped up as a parcel, as part of the 'Brightening up London' campaign. 23 December 2003. AP Photo/Matt Dickens/Orange/Press Association Images.

Page 189
PA.4211952: The Prince of Wales meets Father Christmas as he and the Duchess of Cornwall attend a reception for the 'Not Forgotten' Association at St James's Palace. 7 December 2006. Steve Parsons/WPA Rota/PA.

Page 190
PA.2765976: Footmen carry a giant Christmas card, which was delivered to Buckingham Palace. The card bears an image of a Christmas tree decorated with a thousand photographs of members of the public who also sent festive wishes to Queen. Computer manufacturers Hewlett Packard gave the National Children's Homes charity £1 for each contribution. 15 December 2005. Fiona Hanson/PA Archive/Press Association Images.

Page 191
PA.8400590: Members of the Household Cavalry ride through a snowstorm in central London. 8 January 2003. AP Photo/Ministry of Defence, Pool/AP/Press Association Images.

Page 192
PA.2780542: The Queen in the chapel at Buckingham Palace with choristers from Her Majesty's Chapel Royal, who appear in her Christmas Day broadcast to the Commonwealth. 15 December 2005. Fiona Hanson/PA Archive/Press Association Images.

Page 193
PA.8598598: Queen Elizabeth II distributes Maundy money to pensioners at Derby Cathedral. 1 April 2010. Darren Staples/PA Archive/Press Association Images.

FOR 30 YEARS *Majesty* magazine has been bringing its readers all they need to know about the royal families of the world. Each issue contains knowledgeable features and beautiful photography, with news and views on the personalities, lifestyles, fashions and homes of royals past and present.

From the births of princes and princesses to fairy-tale royal weddings to jubilee celebrations, *Majesty* provides the full story. Intimate interviews with royalty and those who know them offer a unique insight into their privileged lives.

Majesty records all the important royal engagements and takes an in-depth look at the dramatic history of Britain's monarchs. Month by month it builds into a stunning and authoritative royal collection.

Acknowledgments

Special thanks are due to Annette Prosser, Darren Reeve and Carol Taylor for their invaluable assistance with *Royal Entertaining & Style*.